A Business History of the Bicycle Industry

Carlo Mari

A Business History of the Bicycle Industry

Shaping Marketing Practices

palgrave
macmillan

Carlo Mari
Department of Economics
University of Molise
Campobasso, Italy

ISBN 978-3-030-50562-2 ISBN 978-3-030-50563-9 (eBook)
https://doi.org/10.1007/978-3-030-50563-9

This Palgrave Pivot imprint is published by the registered company Springer Nature Switzerland AG
The registered company address is: Gewerbestrasse 11, 6330 Cham, Switzerland

Preface

Bicycles are manufactured objects made available almost everywhere by a complex web of makers, assemblers, suppliers, distributors and retailers, which are generally referred to as the bicycle industry. This industry started as a local activity in Europe, rapidly became an international sector mainly through imports and exports, and lastly, it evolved into a global industry. This is only a vague and very partial description of the bicycle industry. But, what do we actually know about this industry? The answer is that our knowledge base is very limited and the reason behind it is the marginal role played by bicycle research. Bicycles and, in turn, bicycle research are not considered as a serious endeavour. As a result, several topics about the bicycle world are almost completely neglected, particularly the understanding of the bicycle industry.

Current research on bicycle spans different disciplinary domains and covers various topics: For instance, transportation studies deal with engineering and planning issues, sociology of sport focuses on professional road racing, medical approaches to cycling examine the positive effects of pedalling, sociology of technology researches the evolution of bicycle technology and history covers topics partially overlapping with sports and technology. The bicycle industry is generally neglected, despite its significant contribution to the system of *velomobility* (Horton, Cox, & Rosen, 2007, p. 2). Ultimately, the bicycle firms are the organizations that provide the manufactured objects, which enable people to ride for different purposes.

This book intends to remedy this state of affairs offering a contribution to a better understanding of the bicycle industry from the perspective of the firm. Its focus is on the history of marketing practices within the bicycle industry, thus blending the historical and the marketing perspectives. The book aspires to answer the following questions: What did marketing mean for the bicycle industry? How did the bicycle industry carry out its marketing activity? The analysis of marketing practices within bicycle firms has implications for both the mobility based on cycling and the reconstruction of the history of marketing practices. The former area refers to the impact that marketing decisions, made by bicycle firms, might have on fostering the use of bicycle for both utility and leisure purposes. The latter area deals with the contribution of the bicycle industry in shaping marketing practices employed across various industries, particularly the automobile industry.

The book is not a global history of the bicycle industry in the strict sense of covering the entire world, nor does it offer portraits of individual countries. Rather, this book attempts to put together scattered pieces and fill in holes to create a synthetic picture of key themes about the bicycle industry. The book is both chronological and thematic. The approach has been necessarily selective given that no useful records of the bicycle industry is available. The historical approach chosen in this book builds upon official statistics and highlights gaps and detects inconsistencies in the way statistics are developed across countries, a flaw that limits the comparability of data. The book reconstructs the industry marketing practices that influenced many other industries, including the automobile and provides an empirical evidence on one of the leading bicycle producers across the globe.

The book is organized into four chapters. The first chapter examines the manufacturing of bicycles. A bicycle is a product made from a complex set of activities based on various technologies and materials. The chapter reconstructs the history of bicycle fabrication as intertwined with the principle of interchangeable parts and the influence exercised on the automobile industry. The chapter expands its focus from how a bicycle is manufactured to the key categories of firms participating in the business system adopted within the bicycle industry.

The second chapter discusses the data available to understand the bicycle market. The chapter is a journey into the bicycle statistics available to emphasize current drawbacks and limitations. A selection of five statistics is presented through examples based on primary and secondary data drawn from several countries including the United Kingdom or Italy. It focuses on a set of key variables employed to measure the performance of the bicycle industry in the domestic and international context.

The third chapter examines the bicycle marketing focusing on its three pillars, which consist of understanding customers through market segmentation, designing a market offering for those customers who bicycle firms choose to serve and using sports as a marketing tool. For each topic, the chapter discusses the evolution of marketing practice since the birth of the bicycle industry. Furthermore, the chapter is enriched through examples, based on data, showing market segmentation approaches, market offering hierarchies and participation by bicycle firms to key stage-races on the road.

The last chapter provides an extensive exemplification of how a North-American bicycle firm, Cannondale Corporation, managed its marketing activity in Europe during a twenty-year time frame. The analysis deals with its product policy decisions in the Italian market and focuses on how the company created and managed variety in its product lines, and which dimensions of variety were employed.

Piano di Sorrento, Italy — Carlo Mari

Reference

Horton, D., Cox, P., & Rosen, P. (2007). Introduction. In D. Horton, P. Cox, & P. Rosen (Eds.), *Cycling and society* (pp. 1–23). Farnham, UK: Ashgate.

Acknowledgments

I would like to thank the following people for helping me in this endeavour: Tony Hadland, Blandine Helfre, Jan Králík, Andrew Millward, Piero Nigrelli, Lotta Oudhuis, Ross David Petty, Rita Piloni and Mauro Vegni.

The Bicycle Culture Center (Tokyo, Japan) assisted me in navigating through the statistics of Japanese bicycle market.

The team at Palgrave have provided invaluable support through keeping faith with the project.

On a more personal note, I want to remind how important my family was during the development of the project.

Contents

List of Figures

List of Tables

CHAPTER 1

Understanding the Bicycle as a Product

Abstract A bicycle is an artefact, a product made from a complex set of activities based on various technologies and materials. A bicycle encompasses a long list of pieces that can be arranged to form a product architecture, which helps to understand how a bicycle is fabricated and how the bicycle industry evolved over time. The manufacturing of a bicycle is rooted in the context of other metal-using industries and can be better understood through the hypothesis of technological convergence. The history of bicycle fabrication is also intertwined with the principle of interchangeable parts and the influence exercised on the automobile industry. The chapter expands its focus from how a bicycle is manufactured to the key categories of firms participating in the business system adopted within the bicycle industry.

Keywords Product architecture · Technological convergence · Interchangeable parts · Manufacturing processes · Business system

1.1 A Brief Glance at Four Generations of Bicycles

The history of what we now call *bicycle* is studded with controversial narratives about its origin, inventors, and technical evolution. When was the first bicycle invented? Who was the inventor? Which was the

C. Mari, *A Business History of the Bicycle Industry*,
https://doi.org/10.1007/978-3-030-50563-9_1

country leader in technological innovation? Which were the technical features of the bicycle? How did the bicycle evolve over time? This is a partial list of questions that have often received contentious answers within the community of both learned and scholarly people interested in bicycle history. The study of bicycle history has advanced since the 1990s and some valuable contributions are now available, helping to clarify controversies and broadening the knowledge base. It is not realistic nor consistent with the goal of this book to provide a concise history of the bicycle that would not add anything to the available sources, which instead are specifically focused on building such a history.

The goal of this opening section is to offer a short historical background to emphasize the idea of bicycle evolution over time and its implications for conceptualizing the bicycle as a manufactured product. Before sketching how the bicycle evolved, it makes sense to recall one of the controversies regarding its history and specifically the origin of the English word bicycle. According to bicycle history books (Hadland and Lessing 2014, p. 40; Herlihy 2004, p. 23), the word bicycle appeared in France in 1828 indicating a light cab drawn by a single horse and having two wheels on a single axle. Later in 1867–1868 was used in France and the United States meaning a two-wheeled velocipede. It was also introduced in a British patent granted to J. I. Stassen, filed April 8, 1869 (Josephsson 1902, p. 330).

The transition from the early velocipede to the safety bicycle can be described through the conceptual framework developed under the umbrella of a social constructivist approach to technology studies, usually identified with the acronym SCOT. The proponents of such an approach (Pinch and Bijker 1984) see the developmental process of a technological artefact as a search for a solution to a problem recognized by the various social groups involved in its production and use (Bijker 1995, p. 32). It means that a relevant social group (such as the bicycle riders at the time) shares the same set of meanings, attached to the bicycle, and perceives a problem concerning that artefact that needs to be addressed. A range of solutions can be identified through a process based on an alternation of variation and selection among designs. The relevant social groups select some of the problems for further attention, then a variety of solutions are generated, some of these solutions are then selected, which subsequently generate new artefacts (Bijker 1995, p. 51). This evolutionary process changes the artefact's meaning attributed to the bicycle by the relevant social group, whether the solution is implemented or not. The process continues until when all the problems attached to an artefact by various relevant social groups are overcome and a dominant design is institutionalized. The social construction of technology as a method for analysing the history of technologies is not without critiques (Humphreys 2005), but despite them, it is still a valuable model for understanding the multidirectional and complex process of technological innovation.

The present-day bicycle has undergone changes across four generations of bicycles since the 1810s to the late 1890s. These changes are linked to the problems perceived by the relevant social groups concerned with the bicycle and are the results of the developmental process aimed at introducing a new design.

The first generation of bicycles is broadly called the *early velocipede*, also known as draisine or hobbyhorse as a nickname (Hadland and Lessing 2014, p. xvii). It was introduced in Germany in 1817 and made of wood and iron tyres. The rider sat nearly erect and propelled the machine by pushing off the ground with one foot, then the other, as if running (Herlihy 2004, p. 21). Wheels were equal in size and the seat height made easier for the rider to put his feet on the ground (Hadland and Lessing 2014, p. 12). The more fundamental problems recognized by its users were the lack of comfort, the force needed to steer it, and the muddy feet (Bijker 1995, p. 25). The latter problem refers to the road conditions at the time when mud was very frequent and rider's feet were inevitably covered by it. The revision of the draisine gave birth to the second generation of bicycles called the *cranked velocipede*, also known as boneshaker as a nickname. It first appeared in France between 1866 and 1868. This new artefact was similar to the early velocipede, except for cranks attached to the axle of the front wheel. These cranks were pushed by the feet, thus enabling the rider to sit without walking in the mud. Initially, the cracked velocipedes had wooden wheels with iron hoop tyre, which made them noisy on paved roads and subject to sideslip. By 1869, some makers were offering rubber or leather coverings for the iron rims (Hadland and Lessing 2014, p. 59). The front wheel was bigger than the rear wheel and the seat was about one metre from the ground. The cranked velocipedes addressed the problems of the early velocipedes, but were affected by further problems recognized by other relevant social groups. Specifically, the tendency to push one's body backward and away from the pedals when the going became heavy and more force was needed, and the speed problem (Bijker 1995, pp. 28–30). The speed was limited by the pedalling cadence and the wheel diameter as the cranks were directly connected to the front wheel, consequently the only way to realize a greater speed over the ground was to increase the diameter of the front wheel (Berto 2006, p. 21). The answer to these problems was a new generation of bicycles called *high-wheeler*, also known as ordinary or penny-farthing as a nickname. It appeared in France in 1868–1869 and adopted in Britain and United States in the 1870s. The rider sat almost directly over the large front wheel that had a diameter between 43 and 60 inches. The rear wheel was smaller and the saddle height about 1.30 metre. The search for speed had become so important that the trend of enlarging the front wheel continued, and this made it necessary to move the saddle in order to keep pedals within reach of the feet (Bijker 1995, p. 43). The main problem perceived by both users and non-users of the high-wheeler was safety. Any sudden obstruction to the motion of the bicycle frequently had the effect of sending the rider over the handlebar. This element of insecurity soon led to the introduction of other designs of bicycles (Sharp 1896, p. 150).

Several solutions were developed to address this issue roughly in the same period from the late 1870s to the 1880s, but one became known as the fourth generation of bicycles and was called *safety bicycle*. It was invented in 1879, but attained popular favour in 1885 when British cycle makers show the new design to the public for the first time. The Rover, produced in Coventry by John Kemp Starley and William Sutton, was the first true safety bicycle, even though it took two years and three models to evolve into the definitive design of 1886 (Berto 2006, p. 38). The safety bicycle was based on the idea of applying drive to one wheel and steering the other, rather than trying to drive and steer the same wheel (Hadland and Lessing 2014, p. 156). It was a low wheeled bicycle with a saddle height of about one metre, a chain-driven rear wheel, equal-sized wheels, and a triangulated frame. This design formed the prototype of the modern rear-driving bicycle. It had the following advantages: the lower centre of gravity made it safer because it could not tilt forward and the foot could be put to the ground; the riding position was at the same time comfortable and efficient; the weight of the rider was better distributed between the two wheels, which was better for hill climbing and for descending; the bicycle with the chain drive could be geared up or down to suit the rider's needs (Ritchie 2018, p. 181). Table 1.1 provides a comparative analysis of some basic technical features that distinguish each generation of bicycles (Hadland and Lessing 2014; Berto 2006; Minetti et al. 2001).

Table 1.1 Technical data across four generations of bicycle

	Early velocipede	*Cranked velocipede*	*High-wheeler*	*Safety bicycle*
Year	1817	1866–1868	1868–1869	1885
Front wheel diameter (inch)	27	32–36	43–60	30
Rear wheel diameter (inch)	27	29	17–30	30
Tyres	Metal	Metal/solid rubber	Solid rubber	Pneumatic
Saddle height (metre)	0.86	0.99	1.31	1.01

The design of 1886 was further changed through incremental improvements to address the problem of vibration and of going faster on level ground and uphill. In the late 1880s, the invention of the pneumatic tyres by John Boyd Dunlop improved both speed and comfort over the solid rubber tyres. The pneumatic technology was, in turn, further developed through the detachable tyre principle, the repairable tyre principle, and improved valves. The problem of speed, particularly when taking account of factors such as gradients and wind direction (Hadland and Lessing 2014, p. 221), was addressed through the development of a multi-speed gearing mechanism. The first attempts to design a transmission were conducted between the late 1900s and 1910s. In the 1920s, in France and Italy, some small manufacturers created reliable and effective derailleurs that could be retrofitted, which is installed on existing bicycles (Berto 2006, p. 95). The derailleur came of age and became completely practical in the 1930s (Berto 2006, p. 142).

The safety bicycle has become the dominant design and its characteristics are taken for granted as the essential ingredients of the artefact called bicycle nowadays. The introduction and widespread adoption of the safety design gave an immense impetus to the bicycle industry. The safety bicycle was manufactured in large quantities in Europe and United States since the late 1890s. It played a key role in the evolution of the bicycle industry and, consequently, it is useful to deepen its meaning as a product built through a manufacturing technology. The starting point is to decompose a bicycle.

1.2 Decomposing a Bicycle

What is a bicycle? This is not a trivial question as someone, not taking very seriously the bicycle, might think. A bicycle is a multidimensional object that has social lives. It means that its forms, uses and trajectories are intertwined in complex ways with people's lives (Vivanco 2013, p. 41). Its heterogeneous nature encompasses five dimensions interconnected with each other. First, a physical dimension: a bicycle is a material object, a physical thing, an artefact, a tangible product of technology. Its physical properties interact with both the rider and the environment where the bicycle is used. The relationship between a rider's physical characteristics and a bicycle's physical properties is particularly relevant as it influences the performance of the cyclist in pedalling. Second, a functional dimension: a bicycle is an object performing some specific functions, a useful thing that can be used for transportation, leisure and racing purposes. It helps people to move around in urban areas, it contributes to leisure activities such as cycle tourism, it is an essential tool for practicing cycle racing in various disciplines such as road, dirt, and track. Third, an economic dimension: a bicycle is a manufactured object that circulates through complex relationships between producers, labourers, and consumers. These relevant social groups have a vested economic interest in the bicycle. Producers and labourers are interested in the continued proliferation of the artefact, whereas consumers seek a satisfying consumption experience in buying and/or using a bicycle. Fourth, a psychological dimension: a bicycle is an object of cultivated desire. Both bicycle users and potential users might experience a strong longing to a bicycle or a bicycle brand, their fervent desire for such an artefact is not simply based upon needs, but increasingly explained through the passionate feelings and powerful emotions in connection with consumption activities. The psychological dimension is influenced by how producers shape the branding of a bicycle and how people think and talk about a bicycle. Fifth, a temporal dimension: a bicycle has a story to tell with a past, present and future. Its story is connected to its production, exchange, use and eventual disposal. A bicycle has a life course that can be described through a biography based on the following partial list of data: the name of the producer, the place of production, the year of production, the name of the seller, the place of selling, the year of selling, the name of the buyer, the name of the user and the year of disposal.

The five dimensions of a bicycle share what is usually called a product architecture within the manufacturing context (Ulrich 1995). A product, such as a bicycle, is a bundle of components and the architecture is the scheme by which the function of a product is allocated to physical components. The product architecture includes the arrangement of functional elements, the mapping from functional elements to physical components, and the specification of the interfaces among interacting physical components (Ulrich 1995, p. 420). Functional elements refer to what a product does as opposed to what the physical components of the product are. For example, the function for a bicycle, at a most general level of abstraction, consists of a single functional element: transportation (moving from point A to point B). At a more detailed level of abstraction, a collection of functional elements can be specified: support rider weight, make cycling comfortable, make cycling safe and make cycling efficient. The second part of the product architecture refers to physical components and their relationships with functional elements. Each component is a separable physical part and its role is to implement the function of the product. The relationship or mapping between functional elements and components may be one-to-one, many-to-one, or one-to-many. For example, a physical component such as a brake lever contributes to the function of making cycling safe, whereas a bicycle saddle contributes to both functions of supporting rider weight and making cycling comfortable. The third part of the product architecture is the specifications of the physical interfaces among interacting components. Interfaces may adopt a standard protocol used across many different manufacturers and countries or may be based on proprietary protocol. For example, a physical component such as a bottom bracket that interacts with another component called chainring is available in various options, some of them are based on a standard protocol allowing a broader use within the marketplace, whereas others adopt a proprietary protocol which is exclusively compatible with a particular chainring.

The concept of product architecture has been categorized into two typologies: modular and integral. However, it is rather difficult to find real products exhibiting one typology of architecture, most products are somewhere between the extremes of modular or integral (Ulrich 1995, p. 424). A modular architecture allows a one-to-one relationship between functional elements and physical components, and includes de-coupled interfaces between components. Two components are coupled if a change made to one component requires a change to the other in order for the overall product to work correctly (Ulrich 1995, p. 423). An integral architecture includes a complex (many-to-one, or one-to-many) relationship between functional elements and physical components. Modular architecture adopts standardized components and interfaces making easier to change the product over time as components are highly independent, unlike a tightly integrated product architecture that tends to utilize highly interdependent components designed to work specifically or exclusively with other particular components. A modular architecture can also contribute to the ability to economically create product variety to meet customer needs and desires. The degree of modularity can be increased both by expanding the range of compatible components that, in turn, impacts on the range of possible product configurations, and by uncoupling integrated functions within components (Schilling 2000, p. 318).

On a continuum between modular and integral product architecture, a bicycle lies closer to a modular product. Most of its physical components and interfaces are standardized and exception to this practice is for a small number of components usually available for expensive bicycles. A modular product such as a bicycle can be decomposed into a number of physical components that can be mixed and matched in a variety of configurations. The decomposition or disassembly analysis consists of describing the product concept through its physical components at a different level of detail. It is usually based on a four-level analysis: product, systems, subsystems, and components. Systems and subsystems, also called subassembly, are a collection of components that can be assembled into a unit, and can be subsequently treated as a single component during further assembly of the product (Ulrich 1995, p. 423). There is also a fifth level resulting from a complete disassembly of an artefact, down to the last nut, bolt and washer. This decomposition is to the level of individual piece parts and it is usually shown in exploded view drawings available within the catalogues of some companies manufacturing bicycle components.

A bicycle decomposition is depicted in Figs. 1.1 and 1.2. These figures should be examined together to better grasp the four-level analysis. The fifth level of piece parts is omitted for the sake of clarity. This disassembly regards a present-day bicycle descending from the safety bicycle of the 1920s and it is based on various sources (Barnett 2000; Berto 2006; Downs 2005; Grew 1921; Hadland and Lessing 2014; Jones 2005; Oliver and Berkebile 1974; Sharp 1896; Takeuchi 1991; Ueda 1981; Wilson

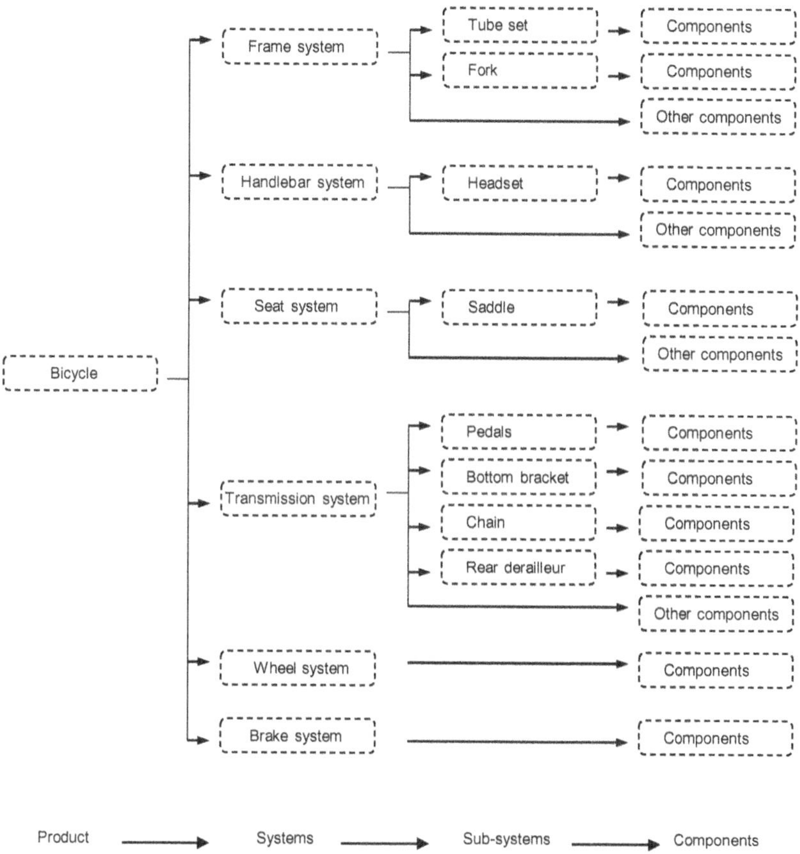

Fig. 1.1 Bicycle decomposition

and Papadopoulos 2004). Such a bicycle includes six systems: frame, handlebar, seat, transmission, wheel and brake.

The frame system contributes more than any other bicycle components to the safety, comfort and performance of the rider. It is the main component onto which the other components are attached. Its design reflects decisions about weight, strength, stiffness, geometry and cost, all of which are influenced heavily by the materials used (Snow et al. 2009). It includes two subsystems and further components: tube set, fork and dropouts (Fig. 1.2). A typical tube set consists of all of the structural

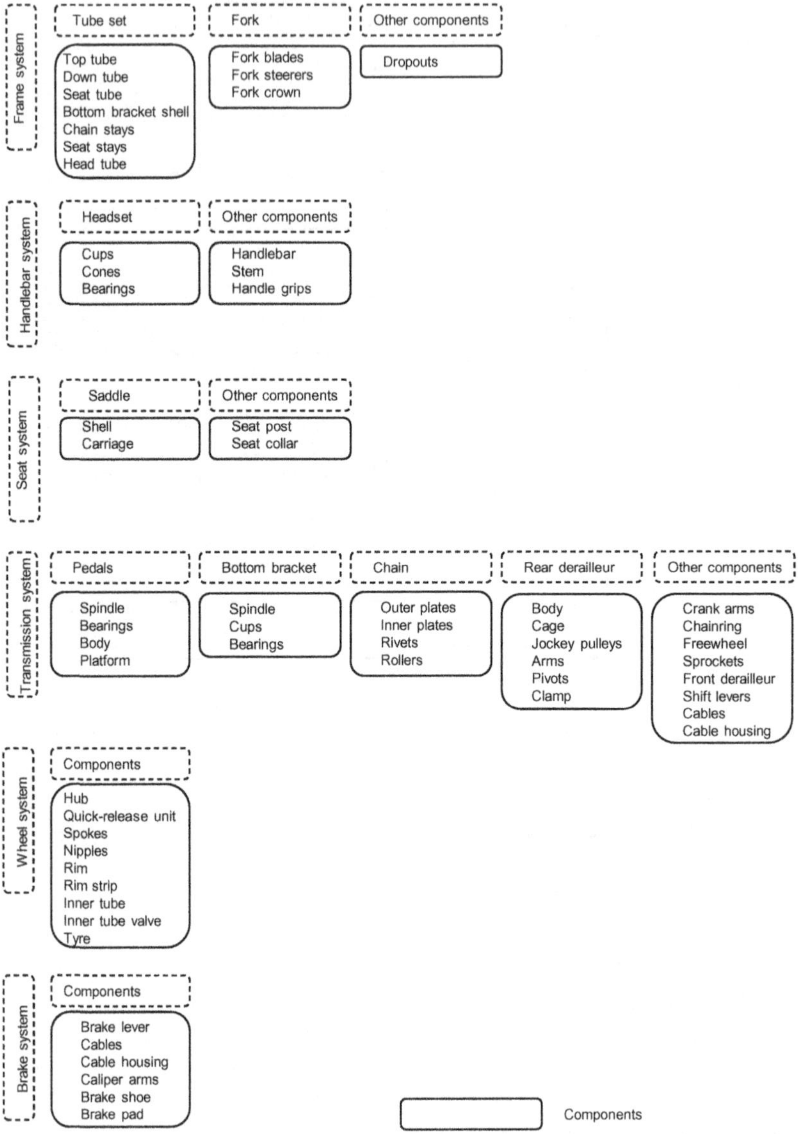

Fig. 1.2 Partial list of bicycle components

tubes required to build a bicycle frame, and its most common form is the diamond frame which includes two triangles. The main triangle composed of the head tube, the top tube, the down tube and the seat tube, and the rear triangle composed of the seat tube and paired chain stays and seat stays. Despite the common practice to use the name diamond, it is slightly misleading as very few bicycles have had a frame that, viewed on elevation, is a true diamond or rhombus, that is a quadrilateral with four equal sides (Hadland and Lessing 2014, p. 160). The frame system is completed with the fork subsystem, used to turn and allow the rider to control the bicycle, and the dropouts which are the slots in the rear triangle and fork where the wheel axles attach. The handlebar system includes a headset subsystem and further components. The headset is the bearing assembly that connects the fork to the frame and allows the fork to rotate inside the head tube (Barnett 2000, p. 2). Handlebar, stem and handle grips are the components that support the rider's hands and allow to control the bicycle. The seat system is composed of a saddle subsystem and further components. The saddle supports the greatest portion of the rider body weight when pedalling, and seat post and seat collar hold the saddle and secure inside the seat tube of the frame (Jones 2005, p. 167).

The transmission system encompasses two functions: to transmit power from the rider's feet and to do so in a way that enables the rider's limbs to move in as near optimum a manner as possible (Wilson and Papadopoulos 2004, p. 311). A transmission system is the connection between a bicycle's power source and the driving wheel. It is also called a drive train system. It includes four subsystems and further components. The pedals subsystem supports the rider's foot and acts as the pushing surface for the foot.

The bottom bracket subsystem is the bearing assembly that allows the cranks to rotate. The chain subsystem connects the front chainrings to the rear sprockets. It is a loop of links made of repeating pairs of outer plates and inner plates, held together by rivets. A roller separates the pair of inner plates (Jones 2005, p. 88). The rear derailleur subsystem moves the chain between the selection of gears on the rear wheel, it works by pushing or derailing the chain from one sprocket to another. Other components complete the drive train: the front derailleur moves the chain from one chainring to another by applying pressure to the side of the chain; the sprockets, also known as cogs or pinions, mesh with the chain and drive the rear wheel and bicycle forward; the chainrings are sprockets attached to the right crank arm that help the transmission of human power to the chain; the crank arms are levers turned by the rider's feet that connect the pedals to the bottom bracket.

The wheel system's function is to convey a load with low resistance when a bicycle rolls forward (Wilson and Papadopoulos 2004, p. 207). This system includes a set of components that allow a smooth ride of a bicycle as one of them (that is the tyre) is the outer portion of the wheel which actually touches the ground. The brake system has a twofold function: to improve bicycle handling and to control speed. It encompasses some components for both the front and rear brake.

The artefact decomposition described through Figs. 1.1 and 1.2 is shared by most types of bicycle, however, there are some differences in the list of components, not shown here, regarding particular bicycles such as the All-Terrain Bicycle (ATB), also known as MounTain bike (MTB) or off-road bicycle, that do not affect the four-level analysis. Moreover, some categories of bicycles had and still have further components such as mudguards, lamps, and bags which are classified as accessories and not included within the previous analysis.

Decomposing a bicycle helps to understand the various components needed to build it and provides some hints on the number of piece parts in a bicycle. The latter topic is not easy to address as it is one of the controversies surrounding the history of the bicycle. According to two sources of the late 1890s, the individual parts of a bicycle were 800 in a man's bicycle and 1000 in a woman's bicycle (Norcliffe 1997, p. 270), or 800 separate pieces (Herlihy 2004, p. 277). Norcliffe cited a British magazine of 1894 and Herlily a British magazine of 1896 in which there was an interview to Albert A. Pope, an American bicycle maker, who was in London for a business trip and provided the data about the number of parts contained in the bicycle manufactured by his company. Another source (Lloyd-Jones and Lewis 2017, p. 157) indicates that the bicycle made by Raleigh, the British bicycle maker, consisted of 1411 parts and if fitted with a Sturmey-Archer gear 1515 parts, during 1920–1934. This information is consistent with a further source (Babaian 1998, p. 41) that cited a British book of bicycle history published in 1955. A safety bicycle consisted of about 300 major components made up of some 1500 individual parts, and the chain alone had over 500 pieces. Wilson (1973, p. 88) indicates that the average bicycle has well over 1000 individual parts, but he did not mention any source for this information. In Japan, during the 1930s, a bicycle consisted of some 200 different parts (Takeuchi 1991, p. 151). A study of the bicycle industry claims that a bicycle may require as many as 200 different components (Mody et al. 1991, p. 20). The most detailed source is an article published, in 1923, by a French magazine that was the official bulletin of bicycle and car makers of Saint-Étienne (Anonymous 1923, pp. 30–31). This town was the centre of the French bicycle industry and it is often referred to as the French Coventry. The article provides a complete disassembly of a bicycle to the level of individual piece parts and the result is 1427 components excluding the accessories. It is possible to know the number of components for each system: frame 51, handlebar 79, seat 34, transmission 844, wheel 347 and brake 72. The drive train system is the most complex component, it has about 60% of the total number of parts followed by the wheel system which has about 25% of the parts of a bicycle. Presumably, the differences between the number of parts of each source depend on both the level of detail at which the components are considered and the evolution of the bicycle over time. The number of components changes at each level of the decomposition analysis: at a higher level (that is, more aggregated) the number is small whereas it increases at a lower level (that is, less aggregated).

The degree of modularization of a bicycle and the possibility to decompose the product in different levels of aggregation have a direct impact on bicycle maker's decisions regarding both component standardization and product variety. These decisions, in turn, affect the manufacturing process used to produce a bicycle and how the industry structure evolves over time. The manufacturing technology is the next step in understanding the bicycle as a product.

1.3 Manufacturing a Bicycle

The production of a bicycle is rooted within the context of other metal-using industries, particularly those already experienced in the production of durable goods requiring small, even intricate, mechanisms and parts (Harrison 1985, p. 51). There is a historical trajectory that links the manufacturing of a bicycle to the production of small firearms, sewing machines, and automobiles. The relationship between these industries can be understood through the hypothesis of *technological convergence* developed by Rosenberg (1963). He studied the industrialization of the American economy focusing on the role played by the capital goods industries, and more particularly the machine tool sector, in introducing and in diffusing technological change. His argument is that machine tools firms appeared as adjuncts to factories specializing in the production of a final product (Rosenberg 1963, p. 418). They worked with manufacturers in various industries to overcome production problems relating to metalworking. As each problem was solved, new knowledge went back into the machine tools firms, which then could be used for solving production problems in other industries (Hounshell 1984, p. 4). Both machinery producing and metal-using sectors showed common processes, initially in the refining and smelting of metal ores, subsequently in foundry work whereby the refined metals are cast into preliminary shapes and then in the various machining processes through which the component metal parts are converted into final form preparatory to their assembly as a finished product (Rosenberg 1963, p. 423). These industries were technologically convergent because there was a close relationship built on a technological basis, regardless of the final product manufactured by each of them. The manufacture of a wide range of products depended upon common metalworking processes, and the machine tool industry originated as a response to the machinery needs of a succession of particular industries making consumer durable goods or other capital goods. The machine tool industry was instrumental both in the initial solution of technological problems and in the rapid transmission and application of newly learned techniques to other uses (Rosenberg 1963, p. 425). The centre of technological convergence was the machine tool industry that performed two tasks: first, it developed or improved new skills and processes in response to problems that arose in particular industries; second, it transferred those new skills and processes to technologically related industries. The machine tool industry may be considered a pool or reservoir of skills and technical knowledge which are employed throughout the entire machine-using sectors of the economy (Rosenberg 1963, p. 426).

Initially, around 1820, the production of machine tools was undertaken by textile firms and arms makers on an ad hoc basis as there was no separately identifiable machine tool sector. These industries were both producers and users of machine tools designed to address the special requirements and specifications of their own manufacturing processes (Rosenberg 1963, p. 417). Textile firms produced heavier, general-purpose machine tools such as lathes, planers and boring machines, whereas arms makers needed lighter, more specialized high-speed machine tools such as turret lathes, milling machines and precision grinders (Rosenberg 1963, p. 419). Other industries played a similar role during the second half of 1800, particularly the manufacturers of sewing machines, bicycles and automobiles. Their evolution is intertwined with the growth of independent machinery-producing firms that occurred in a continuing sequence of stages roughly between the years 1840–1880. This historical sequence began with the small arms industry that impacted the production processes of the sewing machines industry, which, in turn, affected the manufacturing of the bicycle industry that, finally, influenced the technology used by the automobile industry. These sectors were related on a technological basis and each time a solution to the technical problems of a single industry was achieved, it became available for applications in other industries via the machine tool industry which acted as an agent of transmission (Fig. 1.3).

The starting point was the firearms industry during the first half of the nineteenth century when the United States Ordnance Department laid the foundation of a basic aspect of modern manufacturing, the interchangeability of parts (Hounshell 1984, p. 3). The Ordnance Department was an army bureau created in 1812 to inspect and distribute military stores, which in 1815 was in charge of controlling the Springfield and Harpers Ferry armouries, both federally owned arms plants (Hounshell 1984, p. 33). The army bureau spent a lot of money over a forty- or fifty-year period to change the current practice of craft manufacturing

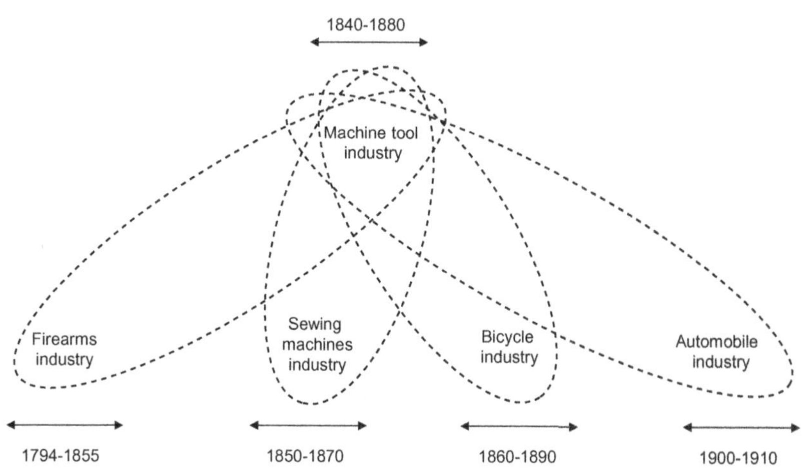

Fig. 1.3 Technological convergence

and reach the uniformity of parts (Hounshell 1984, p. 4). Originally the production of small arms was a handmade activity performed by skilled craftsmen which made each part of the gun by hand, carefully fitting piece to piece. It was a costly, time-consuming, and not very efficient way of fabricating metal parts because no two parts could be made exactly alike. The shortage of skilled gunsmiths and the high cost of production suggested developing an alternative approach to the manufacturing of firearms. The new approach, known as the *American system of manufactures* or *American system of manufacturing*, was based on the manufacturing involving the sequential series of operations carried out on successive special-purpose machines that produce interchangeable parts (Hounshell 1984, p. 15). The key to this system was the complete interchangeability of parts and the ease of attachment them to each other. More specifically, the principle of interchangeable parts was based on the following elements: precision machine tools, precision gauges or other instruments of measurement, uniformly accepted measurement standards and certain techniques of mechanical drawing (Woodbury 1960, p. 247). The system introduced the use of a set of tools called jig and fixture to hold or mount a piece of work. Jigs were simply a metal pattern to guide the machine at the correct angle for turning, drilling or boring and could be moved with the work. Fixtures were fastened to the machine and hold one or more pieces of work in the proper position when more than one machining operation was involved. Fixtures were usually divided into three main categories: holding, measuring, and bending fixture. The idea of interchangeability parts was imported from French military thought and practice which sought to rationalize its armaments in 1765 by introducing standardized weapons with standardized parts. The Ordnance Department through both its establishments and private contractors succeeded in reaching the uniformity of parts using machines by the mid-1850s.

This method of production was adopted and adapted by sewing machine manufacturers, which also hired personnel from small arms firms. The sewing machine industry developed from the 1850s through the 1870s and its machining requirements and processes were similar to those of firearms production. It played a major role as a source of machine tool innovations such as the turret screw machine, the universal milling machine, and the universal grinding machine (Rosenberg 1963, pp. 430–432). These innovations were applied to the production of other metal-using industries, particularly the bicycle sector that became an option for many sewing machine manufacturers, which lost their share of the market, in England and in the United States, and chose the bicycle as a new business. The bicycle industry built its technology of production, from approximately the 1860s through the 1890s, on both the armory practice and the sewing machine manufacturing through the transmission of machine tools and personnel, which played an equally important role in diffusing know-how as they moved from those sectors to bicycle production (Hounshell 1984, p. 5). The requirements of bicycle production revolved around the need for lightness, hardened precision parts and efficient power transmission and friction reduction. The solution to these problems impacted, directly or indirectly, all forms of manufacturing where friction reduction and power transmission were of considerable importance (Rosenberg 1963, p. 434). The bicycle manufacturers were responsible for introducing novel technologies and improved technologies which were made available for numerous new uses. The bicycle industry first employed steel tubing for frame construction, ball bearing, chain drive, differential gearing, pneumatic tyre and tangent-spoked wheels (Harrison 1977, pp. 88–103). It also developed techniques of quantity production utilizing special machine tools, sheet metal stampings and electric resistance (Flink 1990, p. 5). The bicycle manufacturers also stimulated the search for cheaper, lighter and more durable steel which further fostered the rise of the bicycle parts makers (Trescott 1976, p. 55).

The most important direct beneficiaries of the innovations in bicycle production were the automobile makers (Rosenberg 1963, p. 434). Some of them were first bicycle manufacturers such as Humber, Morris, and Rover in Great Britain; Bianchi in Italy; Clément, Darracq, and Peugeot in France; Opel in Germany; Pope, Peerless, Rambler, Winton and Willys in the United States. The transfer of technology from the bicycle sector into automotive production happened during the 1890s and early 1900s through the machine tool industry. The problems of large-scale automobile production involved the extension to a new product of skills and machines not very different from those which had already been developed for bicycles. There were significant continuities regarding the productive processes (Rosenberg 1963, p. 437). The bicycle industry developed both the practice of interchangeable parts and the sheet steel stamping technology which provided the technical basis for the development of mass production within automobile manufacturing in the early twentieth century (Hounshell 1984, p. 190).

The manufacturing processes used to build a bicycle are based on a variety of material conversion technologies that change the physical properties or appearance of materials, or combine them. It means that each workpiece material is altered to create the desired shape through one of the following transformation methods: processes for changing physical properties, processes for changing the shape of materials, processes for machining parts to a fixed dimension, processes for obtaining a surface finish, and processes for joining parts or materials (Hayes and Wheelwright 1984, pp. 167–170; Kalpakjian and Schmidt 2014, p. 16). For example, the starting material (that is the workpiece) may be in the shape of a plate, sheet, bar, rod, wire, or tubing and it can be transformed through a *forming* process that changes its shape to become a part needed to build a bicycle. Another example is the *rolling* process that involves reducing the thickness of a long workpiece by compressive forces applied through a set of rolls. One version of this process, particularly useful in the bicycle industry, is the rotary tube piercing, also known as the Mannesmann process developed in the 1880s. It is a hot-working operation for making long, thick-walled seamless pipe and tubing (Kalpakjian and Schmidt 2014, p. 332).

The production process used in the bicycle industry is a hybrid structure employing both a batch and an assembly line process. It means that items are processed in periodic small lots or batches and the assembly line is used as the final step in a long series of production activities. For example, components parts may be made in a metalworking department, a variety of those components may be combined into subassemblies, and these subassemblies may be assembled and tested using an assembly line (Piloni 1982, p. 116; Hayes and Wheelwright 1984, pp. 177–178). A bicycle is usually an assemble-to-stock product as it combines multiple component parts into a finished product, which is then stocked in inventory to satisfy customer demand. It can also be an assemble-to-order product to customer specification.

The basic elements of the production process involved in building a bicycle are shown in Fig. 1.4. The starting point is the drawing department where bicycles are designed in order to satisfy the needs and wants of potential customers. The outcome of this activity is the list of specific products that will be manufactured and their technical specifications. Identifying such specifications is a key task for deciding which raw materials, such as steel and aluminium, and components have to be bought. The procurement of raw materials and components allows to stock all

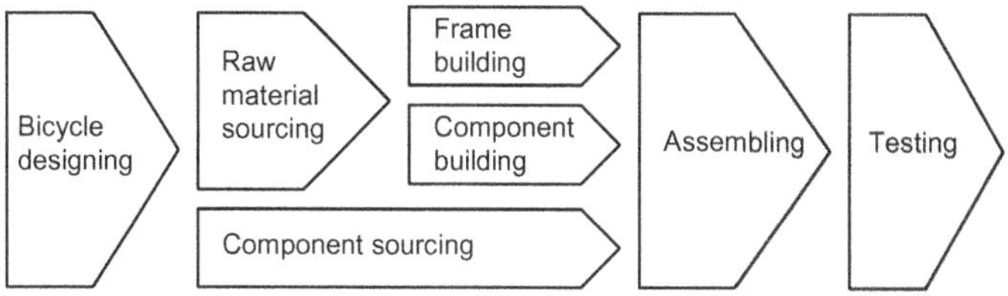

Fig. 1.4 Bicycle production

the items necessary to manufacture the bicycles. Those items are used to build both bicycle frames and some components such as lugs, chainrings, sprockets, hubs, and spokes. A number of finished components are not made but purchased from outside sources such as saddles and tyres. When all the components (including bicycle frame) are available, it is possible to start assembling the complete bicycles, which later are tested for quality and accuracy.

The fabrication of the bicycle frame is the most important activity in the production process and it is also a very distinguishing feature among the bicycle makers, which has significant implications for understanding the historical evolution of the bicycle industry. How is a bicycle frame made? It is possible to make a comparison between the fabrication process of a safety bicycle frame during the nineteenth and twentieth century. Such a process is a sequence of steps, shown in Fig. 1.5, which highlight the main manufacturing technology employed by the bicycle industry. In the 1920s, a bicycle frame was based on steel tubes that could be made in two alternative ways: welded tubing and seamless tubing (Grew 1921, pp. 35–36; Snow et al. 2009, p. 6). Welded tubes started as a flat ribbon of metal that was shaped into the form of a hollow tube and then the joints were welded. This manufacturing process was used, for example, by the British company Raleigh (Lloyd-Jones and Lewis 2017, p. 84) and the Italian company Bianchi (Ministero per la Costituente 1946, p. 279). Seamless tubes started from a bar of metal, called billet, which was transformed through the rotary tube piercing process (Roseo 1912, pp. 75–76). It means that a hole is drilled in the billet that was then pushed through a die and over a mandrel. The internal surface took the form of the mandrel and the external surface took the form of the die. Seamless tubes can be made in different shape and thickness. They are

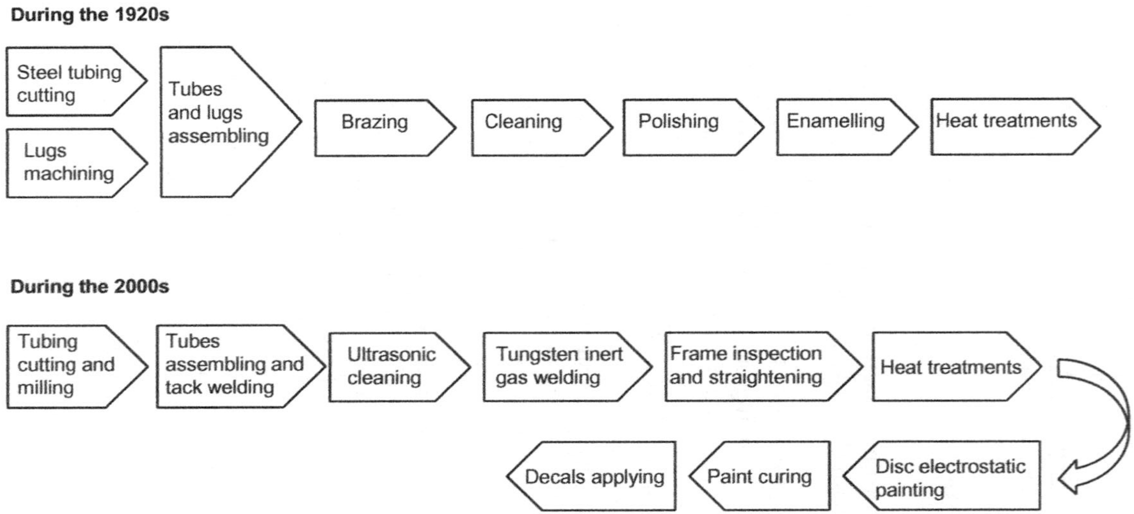

Fig. 1.5 Bicycle frame fabrication

considered to be superior in terms of performance because welding introduces thermal stresses into the metal that compromises its strength. In the 2000s, a bicycle frame was based on both steel and aluminium tubes made as a seamless tube (Bianchi 2005). It was also possible to build a bicycle frame using other materials such as titanium and composites made from carbon fibres.

After manufacturing or buying from an external source the tubes, it is necessary to cut them in various sizes according to the tube set (already explained in Sect. 1.2) and the geometry of each bicycle frame, which was planned to be produced. In the 1920s, tubes also needed a further component, called lug, which was a metal sleeve that surrounds the frame tube at the joint, holding two or more tubes together and strengthening the joint. Each lug added material to the stressed areas (that is the joint), distributing the stresses over a larger area. Lugs were made through machining in the form of castings of stampings. In the 2000s, lugs were rarely used and tubes needed to be shaped on the edges, through milling, so they could easily fit when joined to form the frame. The next step in bicycle frame fabrication is the preliminary assembling of tubes and lugs. This activity is performed using a jig for the correct alignment of the tubes and for keeping the tubes in place. In the 1920s, metal pegs were used to keep in place the lugs, whereas in the 2000s tack welds were used as a temporary weld before applying the final weld.

In the 1920s, the pre-assembled bicycle frame was sent to the brazing shop where the final joint of tubes was done through hearth or liquid brazing (Grew 1921, p. 36; Millward 1999, p. 142), and later to the cleaning shop where the frame went into vats for a bath of corrosive liquid that attacked the rough spelter or, alternatively, it was cleaned through a sand blasting treatment. In the 2000s, the pre-assembled bicycle frame was sent, firstly, to the cleaning shop where a new way of bath based on ultrasound was used and, later, to the welding shop where a new technology, called Tungsten Inert Gas (TIG) welding, replaced the brazing process.

The fabrication of bicycle frame, in the 1920s, encompassed three further steps: polishing, enamelling and heat treatments. Polishing was a process for making the frame surface highly smooth and without any imperfections ready for being painted. Enamelling was a bath of liquid black enamel in vats, which could be repeated three times for high quality bicycle frames. These frames received three coats of thin enamel and were baked, between each application, at a high temperature for a few hours in gas heated stoves (Grew 1921, p. 41). The fabrication of bicycle frame, in the 2000s, encompassed more steps highlighting some technological improvements adopted by the bicycle industry. After a frame was welded, it needed to be inspected for any imperfection that required straightening through a squaring stand. The next step was based on heat treatments to increase the strength properties of bicycle frame. Later, the frame went to the painting shop where a disc electrostatic technology was used to reach a smooth end result. The painted frame was then baked in a curing oven to prepare it for further painting or decals applying. For example, some bicycle frames could receive a further coat through a brushing paint technique or a powder coating. The final step was the application of graphics and decals on bicycle frame.

How a bicycle and its components are manufactured impacts on how the bicycle industry is organized, particularly the behaviour of firms in determining their boundaries. Which is the extent of a bicycle firm's activities in production? Is outsourcing a common practice within the bicycle industry? The next section provides an answer to these questions through the lens of a conceptual tool called the business system.

1.4 Bicycle Industry Structure

The organization and the evolution of the bicycle industry over time are intertwined with both the product architecture and the manufacturing of a bicycle. How a bicycle is decomposed and manufactured helps explaining the structure of the bicycle industry. A key feature for understanding the organization of a generic industry is to focus on the boundaries of a firm, in particular the extent to which a firm is vertically integrated and which activities are no longer internally carried out, but instead it purchases from other firms. This is usually framed as a make-or-buy decision. It means determining what to do internally versus what to outsource in the market (Churn and Ware 2000, pp. 63–64). Vertical boundaries are usually depicted through a sequence of stages or activities, called the vertical chain, performing two distinct types of function: a physical function and a market mediation function. The physical function includes converting raw materials into parts, components and eventually finished goods, and transporting all of them from one point in the chain to the next. Less visible but equally important is market mediation, whose purpose is ensuring that the variety of products reaching the marketplace matches what consumers want to buy (Fisher 1997, p. 107). Vertical integration occurs when these stages are organized within a single firm. The concept of the vertical chain has been studied from various perspectives and called in different ways. For example, in the 1970s French economists introduced the words *filières de production* or *filières industrielles* (Bellon 1984, pp. 111–112), during the 1980s management scholars referred to it as a *business system* (Gluck 1980, p. 26; Buaron 1981, p. 33) or a *value chain* (Porter 1985, p. 33), and in the 1990s US sociologists called it a *global value chain* (Gereffi et al. 2005, p. 79). In this book, the terms business system is preferred to suggest that the stages are interdependent and form a complex unity. A business system is shown as a sequential chart encompassing the key elements of the system by which companies in a given business produce their goods or services and deliver them to the customer. For example, in a technology-based manufacturing company, these elements might be technology, product design, production, distribution, sales and service. At each link of the business system, there are a number of choices management can make about how to conduct the business. Obviously, these are often interdependent: product design will partially constrain the choice of raw materials; decisions on physical distribution will constrain manufacturing capacity and location and vice versa. A business system can differ from industry to industry and frequently even from company to company. It emphasizes the benefits that firms derive in breaking the system into discrete parts to help them look for innovative organizational and managerial practices.

A generic representation of the business system of a firm manufacturing a complete bicycle is shown in Fig. 1.6, it is relatively standard for the industry, but may vary in some essential details from firm to firm. This business system encompasses five stages: (a) market opportunity analysis, which means to conduct some form of market research to understand what consumer want and what competitors are doing in the marketplace; (b) production, which is the set of activities for manufacturing a bicycle as already explained in Sect. 1.3; (c) distribution, which means building a network of intermediaries involved in making bicycles available for consumption; (d) sales, which means managing the relationship with consumers; and (e) post-sales service, which is the activity mainly focused on bicycle repairing. Companies involved in manufacturing a complete bicycle can be broadly categorized as a maker or an assembler. The main difference between them is the frame fabrication that, in the former case, is done in-house, and in the latter case is outsourced to a supplier. The

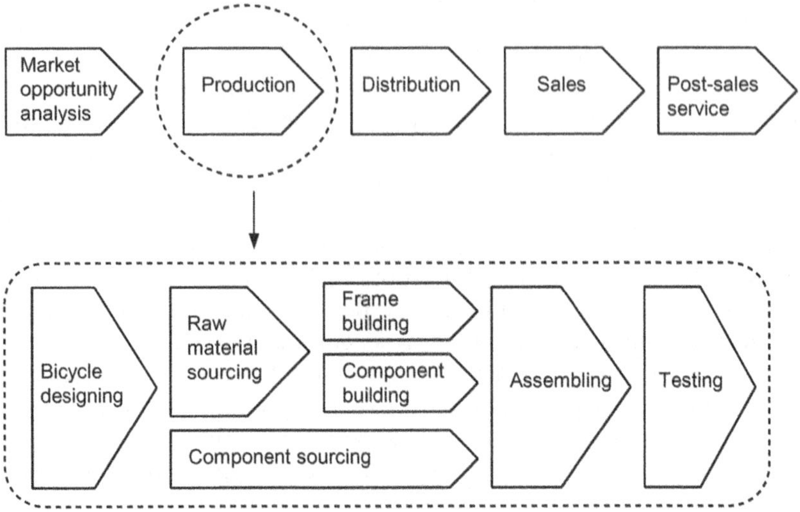

Fig. 1.6 Business system of a bicycle firm

maker is a more vertically integrated firm as it decided to manufacture frame internally, whereas the assembler is completely relying on outside suppliers as it decided to do frame production externally. The choice of manufacturing frame internally or externally has a direct impact on the business system of a firm that changes accordingly to the stages needed to produce a complete bicycle. If bicycle frames are bought from outside sources, the business system will not include the stages associated with frame fabrication. The distinction between makers and assemblers has been a feature of the bicycle industry since its birth and it has become even more marked with the success of the safety bicycle.

Besides makers and assemblers, further companies contribute to the bicycle industry even though they do not manufacture a complete bicycle. These firms are suppliers of components, other than a bicycle frame, which have to be incorporated in a bicycle. It is possible that a maker decides to manufacture internally some components and this choice increases its degree of vertical integration. In some cases, big bicycle makers built a high vertically integrated company such as Raleigh in UK, Bianchi in Italy, and Pope Manufacturing Company in the United States. Raleigh and Bianchi manufactured each component, including the frame, except for chains, saddles, and tyres. Pope Manufacturing Company was also able to produce tyres. A myriad of component manufacturers was, and still is, the backbone of the bicycle industry all over the world. This industry adopted, since its birth, a disintegrated system of production based on specialized capabilities associated with the manufacture of the various components (Galvin and Morkel 2001, p. 32). It was difficult and costly for most of the firms to have the capabilities to manufacture the full range of components that were required to construct a bicycle. Due to the specialized skills necessary in different bicycle manufacturing technologies, it was more efficient to source the components from external suppliers. The consequence is a highly fragmented industry where suppliers have developed specialist capabilities, which make them more competitive than vertically integrated companies. In some cases, such as the Taiwan bicycle industry, suppliers are very specialized, with over 90% manufacturing only one type of component (Chu and Li 1997, p. 63). It is also a common practice that specialist firms or component manufacturers organized themselves in functional tiers, where each first-tier supplier formed a second tier of suppliers under itself. Companies in the second tier were assigned the job of fabricating individual components.

The business system perspective and the categories of maker, assembler, and component manufacturer help to clarify further features of the bicycle industry, which are usually applied to the whole industry regardless of the role played by different firms. Previous studies (Harrison 1977; Millward 1999) have highlighted the following characteristics: bicycle industry is not regarded as a capital-intensive industry, the technology for bicycle production is relatively simple, accessing the industry is easy due to low barriers of entry, a very common practice is copying other firm's products, and the market has a seasonal pattern that affects how companies organize their own activity. The first three statements are true if applied to assemblers, but are more questionable in regard to makers or component manufacturers. It is easier to start a firm whose activity is exclusively bicycle assembly. A new entrepreneur requires a limited amount of both technological capabilities and money to assemble bicycles. There are no particular barriers that prevent starting a new business whose goal is to assemble bicycles. Instead, it is quite a different situation if someone decide to become a bicycle maker or a component manufacturer. The technological capabilities required are more demanding and so it is the investment to begin the activity. Consequently, there are barriers that make the access less easy in comparison with hindrance facing an assembler. The practice of copying products of each other is common within the whole bicycle industry and involves the three categories of firms (maker, assembler and component manufacturer). This practice is a direct effect of the division of labour and increasing specialization that generates a fragmented industry. This way of organizing the system of production is aimed at creating economies of scale through standardized components, including bicycle frames, which makes easier copying other firm's products. The seasonal pattern of the bicycle market involves the whole industry and has an annual cycle. This way of doing business characterizes the industry since its birth (Roseo 1912, pp. 214–215) and is still in place nowadays as described in the annual report of a Dutch bicycle firm (Accell 2019, p. 6). The cycle has an almost fixed pattern every year and lasts for twelve months from September to August of the next year. Each firm that manufactures complete bicycles has to deal with two offerings of bicycle simultaneously. In September of each year, the current offering of bicycles is launched in the marketplace and, at nearly the same time, the firm starts thinking about the new offering that will be launched in twelve-month time, based on preliminary data drawn from the current offering. September is also when bicycle firms have to begin to negotiate sales agreements with their own network of dealers, particularly the decisions focused on sales goals (how many bicycles the dealer is going to order) and margins (which is the profit margin granted to the dealer). During the timeline shown in Fig. 1.7, the activities involving both offerings are intertwined in an unceasing cycle that repeats itself every year. The seasonality of the bicycle industry is also connected with weather conditions, which explain why the delivery peak is between February and June, and consumer sales peak is usually in spring and summer seasons, with obvious differences between geographical areas.

The concept of the business system is a useful lens for understanding the evolution of bicycle industry in various countries providing that some data is available. In many instances it is not possible to say for sure whether bicycle firms were actually a maker or an assembler. The following is a sketch of how the bicycle industry evolved in Italy since its inception. The Italian experience shares similarities with other countries that developed a domestic bicycle industry and, therefore, it can help to shed light on the role played by the different categories of firms participating in the industry, regardless of the peculiarities of any geographical context.

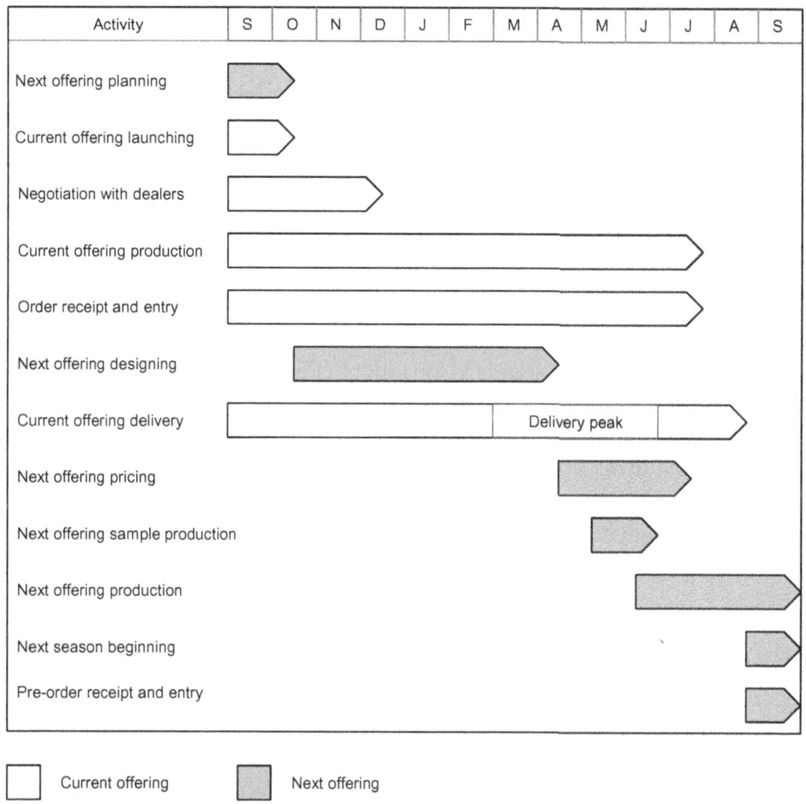

Fig. 1.7 Seasonal pattern of bicycle market

The history of the Italian bicycle industry can be broadly divided into four phases spanning from the 1880s to the present time. Before the 1880s, there were initial attempts to build bicycles in 1867 in the city of Modena, and between 1872 and 1878 in Milan, Bologna and Turin (Vota 1954, pp. 19–20). The first phase, from 1880 to 1890, saw an increasing number of small craftsmen joining the nascent industry. Their businesses were very small and did not specialize in bicycles, but produced or repaired a wide range of mechanical products. They focused on repairing foreign bicycles. Most of those artisans were in the northern part of the country, primarily located in Milan and Turin (Roseo 1912, p. 147). A notable exception was Edoardo Bianchi who run a small mechanical repair shop in Milan and developed the first safety style bicycle in Italy in 1886, inspired by an imported English bicycle (Mari 2015, p. 134). Form his shop he was able to build one of the world's leading and most popular bicycle firms. During the first phase, the contribution of Italian bicycle firms to the business system was limited to the post-sale service stage through their repairing activity. Other stages were carried out by foreign companies exporting bicycles to Italy.

In the second phase, between 1890 and 1900, the industry experienced a significant growth, made possible because the financial needs of those firms were limited as most of them bought components that were assembled to sell standard products (Piloni 1982, pp. 9–10). The Italian market was dominated by bicycles imported from abroad, principally England, Germany, France and the US (Roseo 1912, pp. 164–167). Italian bicycle firms broadened the number of activities carried out within the business system, and were involved in understanding the market, assembling complete bicycles, distributing, selling and repairing them. The production stage, as depicted in Fig. 1.8, encompassed an assembly

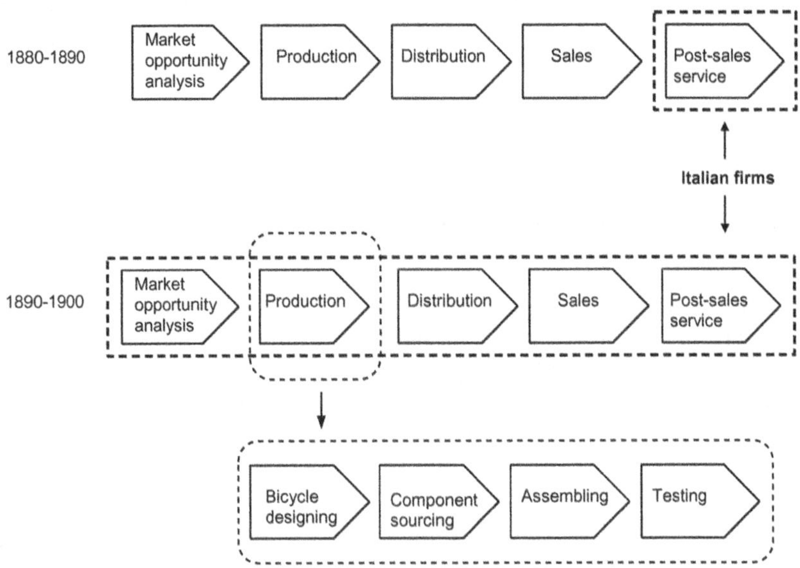

Fig. 1.8 Business system of Italian bicycle industry 1880–1900

activity based on designing a bicycle offering, sourcing the components needed to assemble it, and testing the complete bicycles.

The third and longest phase began in the 1900s and lasted until the 1970s. Domestic production of complete bicycles began to take off due to the increase in bicycle sales in Italy and the start of an export trade (Roseo 1912, pp. 183–189). Although production was still dispersed in a myriad of small workshops and craftsmen, some firms started to access external financial sources that led to the birth of a few joint-stock companies (Piloni 1982, pp. 70–72). Most of the bicycle components were manufactured in Italy and the industry was highly fragmented. Five distinct groups of firms were involved in the industry: a very few vertical integrated companies that carried out all the manufacturing processes on their own premises and sold complete bicycles, some makers of bicycle frames that bought components from other firms and sold complete bicycles, a large number of small assemblers that bought everything was needed for building a bicycle from outside sources and sold complete bicycles, a high number of local artisans mainly involved in bicycle repairing and very limited bicycle assembly, and some small and medium firms that carried out the fabrication of components and spare parts (ANCMA 1953, p. 362; Piloni 1982, pp. 18–19). The backbone of the industry was located in three geographical areas, specifically, in order of importance, Lombardy, Veneto and Piedmont (ANCMA 1953, p. 363). In 1949 most of the key firms were in Lombardy: 46% of those building complete bicycles and 60% of those manufacturing components (Piloni 1982, p. 58). Milan was the capital of the Italian bicycle industry and the following firms had their headquarters in the city: Bianchi, Legnano, Borghi (whose brand was Olympia), Focesi (whose brand was Gloria), Viscontea, and Taurus. The geography of Italian bicycle industry also included Varese, where Ganna started his firm; Padua, where Rizzato (whose brand was Atala) and Torresini (whose brand was Torpado) built their bicycles; Vittorio Veneto where Carnielli (whose brand was Bottechia) began his business; Bassano del Grappa, where Willier Triestina was active; and Celle Ligure, where Olmo manufactured his bicycles. In the summer of 1920, in Milan, the most important companies founded a national organization to protect its members' commercial interests (Borruso 1996, p. 167). Its acronym was ANCMA (Associazione Nazionale del Ciclo Motociclo e Accessori) and included makers of bicycles, motorcycles and accessories for both kinds of vehicles.

This phase witnessed the coexistence of vertically integrated firms, frame makers, assemblers, craftsmen and specialized suppliers of components. Very few firms had both financial resources and capabilities to manufacture a complete bicycle. Most firms did not find advantageous to internalize activities through formal integration and chose to focus on frame building or assembling. The business system of these five groups of firms highlights some differences as depicted in Fig. 1.9, particularly the missing activities that each category of firms did not carry out at the production stage. Obviously, vertically integrated firms showed the whole range of activities for manufacturing bicycles internally, whereas other firms did not perform some tasks consistently with their choice to buy most or all the components from external sources. For example, assemblers outsourced everything, including bicycle frames; and local craftsmen usually did not have enough capabilities to design a bicycle. At the same time, other stages of the business system, such as marketing opportunity analysis, distribution, sales, and post-sales service were carried out at a different degree of completeness and professionalism by each group of firms. For example, a vertically integrated company was able to develop resources in any of the stages, whereas an artisan was mainly devoted to bicycle repairing and, consequently, other stages of the business system were compressed or completely missing. In a similar vein, component manufacturers performed all the stages, even though they did not build and sell bicycles. Their activities were performed in relationship with other firms within the industry, for example, their post-sales service was available to consumers through bicycle dealers.

The fourth and last phase is from the 1980s to the present and is characterized by the progressive decrease in the number of both vertically integrated firms and frame manufacturers. Fierce competition from foreign countries, particularly from Far East, drove this shift in the Italian bicycle industry. At the present time, the whole industry is made up of assemblers and component manufacturers. This change affected also the long-standing tradition of fabricating high quality steel frames which are, now, almost completely disappeared, except for a few artisanal makers that build a limited number of custom frames. The business system of this phase overlaps with the one depicted in Fig. 1.9. The key difference, not shown in the chart, is that there is only one vertically integrated firm in Italy, its name is Bianchi and it was acquired by a foreign group in 1997. The main category of firms within the industry is now the assembler, which has become synonymous with a bicycle company.

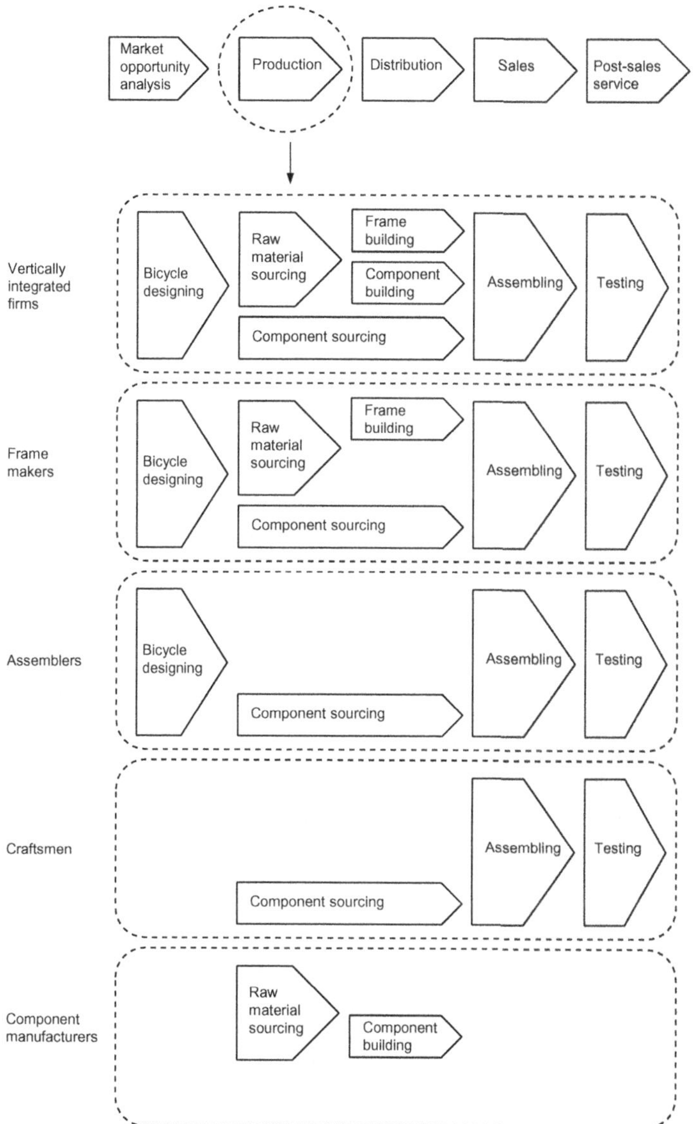

Fig. 1.9 Business system of Italian bicycle industry 1900–1970s

The Italian bicycle industry evolved through an import-substitution industrialization model aimed at replacing foreign imports with domestic production. Both complete bicycles and components were imported. The former were what consumers wanted and the infant industry was not ready to provide yet. The latter were the easiest way to establish a form of industry through the assembly of bicycles, which was the manufacturing technology most accessible for starting a firm. The accumulated learning during the import years enabled the industry to expand its capacity quickly. From the 1880s to 1907, the import of foreign bicycles was the main source for the Italian marketplace, particularly the British products. In 1908, the domestic production took off, and the import of bicycles from other countries decreased accordingly (Piloni 1982, p. 49). The import-substitution model was the same path followed by other countries both in Europe and Asia, such as France, the Netherlands, Japan, China and Taiwan. France is credited with initiating the bicycle industry in the 1860s, but it lost its advantage when UK assumed the major position in bicycle production at the beginning of the 1870s and was to be the main supplier to world markets for the following twenty years (Millward 1999, pp. 72–73). One of the earliest large-scale bicycle firm in France was the Manufacture française des armes et cycles (MFAC) based in Saint-Etienne, a town and region that was a key centre of the French bicycle industry (Dauncey 2012, p. 79). MFAC was founded in 1885 and was initially only concerned with the sale and repair of imported British bicycles, but in 1888 started producing bicycles for the growing market and it became the first vertically integrated firm in its country. From the late 1890s to the mid-1920s, in Saint-Etienne area the bicycle industry was organized around a small number of large firms and a myriad of subcontractors providing components. The Dutch market imported bicycles from UK, Germany and US since the 1880s until 1925. Afterwards, the local industry began to manufacture complete bicycles through domestic makers and assemblers (Tjong Tjin Tai et al. 2015, p. 21). The bicycle industry in Japan inherited from UK complete bicycles, components, and most importantly the first vertically integrated firm. The imports from UK started in the 1890s and lasted until the 1910s (Takeuchi 1981, p. 38). Japanese entrepreneurs developed a method of bicycle assembly known as *set fitting* or knock-down system. It meant that Japanese firms imported unassembled components in sets that were put together to form complete bicycles. In 1910, in the city of Kobe, a British bicycle firm established a branch factory that was instrumental in developing the native industry in Japan (Takeuchi 1981, p. 46). The Japanese industry used extensively the putting-out system of production based on complex multilayered subcontract relationships. Each bicycle component or, in some cases, manufacturing process was entrusted to a subcontractor that could be committed to just one company and heavily rely on family labour (Takeuchi 1991, pp. 159–160; Ueda 1981, p. 14). China imported bicycles from UK, Germany and Japan between 1879 and the 1920s. Its native bicycle industry was connected to a Japanese entrepreneur who started three firms in China between 1936 and 1938 (Petty 2001, pp. 198–199). These three firms were confiscated and nationalized by the government in 1949 and the imports ceased because of the Sino-Japanese war and the US trade embargo (Rhoads 2012, pp. 105–106). Since the 1950s, the Chinese government played a key role in developing the domestic bicycle industry through investment for firm expansion, company restructuring and creating zones were foreign investment was permitted. In Taiwan the bicycle industry started later than in other countries and it was greatly influenced by the experience of the Japanese industry (Chen et al. 2009, p. 207). Taiwan imported both complete bicycles and components from Japan between 1946 and 1951, afterwards the government adopted policies that limited imports and the domestic bicycle industry expanded its manufacturing capabilities (Chu and Li 1997, p. 57). The bicycle industry, in Taiwan, consisted primarily of frame makers and component manufacturers. The former fabricated no components except the bicycle frame, the latter were very specialized with each manufacturing a very limited number of products. Component manufacturers became increasingly independent from domestic frame makers, exporting over 50% of their production (Chu and Li 1996, pp. 43–44). In 1969, Taiwan began to export its bicycles to the United States and until the 1980s the industry experienced significant and continuous growth. In the 1970s, Taiwan's bicycle firms went to Japan to learn about standardization of bicycle components, which helped them to improve their technological knowledge. During the 1980s, the government helped bicycle firms to deal with the issue of low-quality products through the development of more advanced manufacturing processes and skills within the whole business system.

1.5 Conclusion

The business system perspective is a fruitful approach to study the evolution of the bicycle industry as it provides a neglected lens to interpret how vertical chains are organized locally and globally. It is particularly useful to highlight the trajectories followed by different categories of companies over time and in various geographical areas. It could also help to envision what the bicycle industry will be like in the future.

The current situation indicates a polarization between assemblers and component manufactures as the best equipped to survive, and perhaps prosper, within the bicycle industry in the coming years. An evident phenomenon is the rise of the so called mega-suppliers in various industries, including the bicycle sector (Donovan 1999, p. 1). Mega-suppliers are big firms manufacturing and assembling entire modular packages such as the transmission system, the brake system, the wheel system or the front and rear suspension. Their approach is different from the traditional supplier of bicycle components for three reasons: they build an integrated system made of many components, rather than providing some single pieces, which contribute to define current and new standards within the bicycle industry; they will likely lead the industry in the technological innovation as their size allows them to invest in research and development, so that the locus of bicycle innovation will be concentrated in a small number of firms; and they can use ingredient-branding as a tool for advertising directly to consumers, which will likely search for a bicycle assembled with a particular brand of components.

Power within the bicycle industry is progressively flowing away from assemblers towards the large component manufacturers. Today, there are two mega-suppliers in the global bicycle industry: a Japanese firm (Shimano) and a US firm (SRAM). An Italian company (Campagnolo) could also be considered a potential mega-supplier, even though its size is smaller than its competitors. Moreover, Campagnolo's offering is narrower than what both Shimano and SRAM are currently manufacturing for the marketplace.

A further impetus for establishing mega-suppliers is the birth of a large market for both pedal electric cycle, or pedelecs, and electric bicycles. The former are bicycles with electric motors that assist riders, the latter can be propelled without pedalling. This new market is incessantly growing in many countries and manufacturers of electric motors, not already involved in the bicycle industry, are providing their offering to bicycle assemblers, which are dependent on using a technology developed by an outside source.

References

Accell Group N.V. (2019). *Accell annual report 2018*. Heerenveen, The Netherlands: Accell Group N.V.

ANCMA. (1953). L'industria del ciclo e del motociclo. In Confederazione Generale dell'Industria Italiana (Ed.), *L'industria Italiana alla Metà del Secolo XX* (pp. 362–368). Rome, Italy: Tipografia del Senato.

Anonymous. (1923). Porquoi une seule maison ne peut-elle fabriquer un vélo dans tous ses détails? Un bel exemple de division du travail. *L'Industrie des Cycles et Automobiles*, Septembre–Octobre, 30–31.

Babaian, S. (1998). *The most benevolent machine: A historical assessment of cycles in Canada*. Ottawa, ON, Canada: National Museum of Science and Technology.

Barnett, J. (2000). *Barnett's manual. Analysis and procedures for bicycle mechanics* (4th ed.). Boulder, CO: Velo Press.

Bellon, B. (1984). La filiera di produzione. *Economia e Politica Industriale, 42*, 109–131.

Berto, F. J. (2006). *The dancing chain. History and development of the derailleur bicycle* (2nd ed.). San Francisco, CA: Van der Plas Publications.

Bijker, W. E. (1995). *Of bicycles, bakelites, and bulbs. Toward a theory of sociotechnical change*. Cambridge, MA: The MIT Press.

Borruso, E. (1996). *Studi di storia dell'industria «milanese» (1836–1983)*. Milan, Italy: Guerini Scientifica.

Buaron, R. (1981). New-game strategies. *The McKinsey Quarterly*, Spring, 24–40.

Chen, Y., Lin, M. J., Chang, C., & Liu, F. (2009). Technological innovations and industry clustering in the bicycle industry in Taiwan. *Technology in Society, 228*(31), 207–217.

Chu, W., & Li, J. (1996). Growth and industrial organization. A comparative study of the bicycle industry in Taiwan and South Korea. *Journal of Industry Studies, 3*(1), 35–52.

Chu, W., & Li, J. (1997). Causes of growth: A study of Taiwan's bicycle industry. *Cambridge Journal of Economics, 21*(1), 55–72.

Churn, J., & Ware, R. (2000). *Industrial organization: A strategic approach*. New York, NY: McGraw-Hill.

Dauncey, H. (2012). *French cycling. A social and cultural history*. Liverpool, UK: Liverpool University Press.

Donovan, D. (1999). *The dawn of the mega-supplier: Winning supplier strategies in an evolving auto industry*. Boston, MA: Bain & Company Inc.

Downs, T. (2005). *The bicycling guide to complete bicycle maintenance and repair for road & mountain bikes* (5th ed.). Emmaus, PA: Rodale Inc.

Fisher, M. L. (1997). What is the right supply chain for your product? *Harvard Business Review*, March–April, 105–116.

Flink, J. J. (1990). *The automobile age*. Cambridge, MA: The MIT Press.

FIV E. Bianchi S.p.A. (2005). *Bianchi factory tour*. Treviglio, Italy: FIV E. Bianchi S.p.A.

Galvin, P., & Morkel, A. (2001). The effect of product modularity on industry structure: The case of the world bicycle industry. *Industry and Innovation, 8*(1), 31–47.

Gereffi, G., Humphre, J., & Sturgeon, T. (2005). The governance of global value chains. *Review of International Political Economy, 12*(1), 78–104.

Gluck, F. W. (1980). Strategic choice and resource allocation. *The McKinsey Quarterly*, Winter, 22–33.

Grew, W. F. (1921). *The cycle industry. Its origin, history and latest developments*. London, UK: Sir Isaac Pitman & Sons Ltd.

Hadland, T., & Lessing, H. E. (2014). *Bicycle design. An illustrated history*. Cambridge, MA: The MIT Press.

Harrison, A. E. (1977). *Growth, entrepreneurship and capital formation in the United Kindom's cycle and related industries, 1870–1914*. PhD thesis, University of York.

Harrison, A. E. (1985). The origin and growth of the UK cycle industry to 1900. *The Journal of Transport History, 6*(1), 41–70.

Hayes, R. H., & Wheelwright, S. C. (1984). *Restoring our competitive edge. Competing through manufacturing*. New York, NY: Wiley.

Herlihy, D. V. (2004). *Bicycle. The history*. New Haven, CT: Yale University Press.

Hounshell, D. A. (1984). *From the American system to mass production 1800–1932. The development of manufacturing technology in the United States*. Baltimore, MD: The Johns Hopkins University Press.

Humphreys, L. (2005). Reframing social groups, closure, and stabilization in the social construction of technology. *Social Epistemology, 19*(2–3), 231–253.

Jones, C. C. (2005). *Big blue book of bicycle repair. A do-it-yourself bicycle repair guide from Park Tool*. Saint Paul, MN: Park Tool Company.

Josephsson, A. (1902). Manufactures: Bicycles and tricycles. In W. R. Merriam (Ed.), *Bulletins: Twelfth census of the United States*, No. 176 (pp. 323–339). Washington, DC: United States Census Office.

Kalpakjian, S., & Schmidt, S. R. (2014). *Manufacturing engineering and technology* (7th ed.). New York, NY: Pearson Education Inc.

Lloyd-Jones, R., & Lewis, M. J. (2017). *Raleigh and the British bicycle industry. An economic and business history, 1870–1960*. London, UK: Routledge.

Mari, C. (2015). Putting the Italians on bicycles: Marketing at Bianchi, 1885–1955. *Journal of Historical Research in Marketing, 7*(1), 133–158.
Millward, A. (1999). *Factors contributing to the sustained success of the UK cycle industry 1870–1939*. PhD thesis, University of Birmingham.
Minetti, A. E., Pinkerton, J., & Zamparo, P. (2001). From bipedism to bicyclism: Evolution in energetics and biomechanics of historic bicycles. *Proceedings of The Royal Society B, 268*(1485), 1351–1360.
Ministero per la Costituente. (1946). *Rapporto della Commissione Economica presentato all'Assemblea Costituente, volume II: Industria, II Appendice alla Relazione (Interrogatori): Interrogatorio dell'ing. Giuseppe Bianchi*. Rome, Italy: Istituto Poligrafico dello Stato.
Mody, A., Sanders, J., Suri, R., Rao, C., & Contreras, F. (1991). *International competition in the bicycle industry: Keeping pace with technological change* (Industry Series Paper, No. 50). Washington, DC: The World Bank Industry and Energy Department.
Norcliffe, G. (1997). Popeism and Fordism: Examining the roots of mass production. *Regional Studies, 31*(3), 267–280.
Oliver, S. H., & Berkebile, D. H. (1974). *Wheels and wheeling. The Smithsonian cycle collection*. Washington, DC: Smithsonian Institution Press.
Petty, R. D. (2001). The rise of the Asian bicycle business: State support and survival strategies. In A. Ritchie & R. Van der Plas (Eds.), *Cycle History 11: Proceedings of the 11th International Cycling History Conference* (pp. 189–204). San Francisco, CA: Van der Plas Publications.
Piloni, R. (1982). *Un settore industriale in sviluppo: L'industria della bicicletta dalla fine dell'Ottocento al 1914*. Master thesis, University of Milan.
Pinch, T. J., & Bijker, W. E. (1984). The social construction of facts and artefacts: or how the sociology of science and the sociology of technology might benefit each other. *Social Studies of Science, 14*(3), 399–441.
Porter, M. E. (1985). *Competitive advantage. Creating and sustaining superior performance*. New York, NY: The Free Press.
Rhoads, E. J. M. (2012). Cycles of Cathay: A history of the bicycle in China. *Tranfers, 2*(2), 95–120.
Ritchie, A. (2018). *Early bicycles and the quest for speed. A history, 1868–1903* (2nd ed.). Jefferson, NC: McFarland & Company.
Rosenberg, N. (1963). Technological change in the machine tool industry. *The Journal of Economic History, 23*(4), 414–443.
Roseo, G. G. (1912). *L'industria e il commercio dei velocipedi nel mondo*. Milan, Italy: Libreria Editrice Milanese.
Schilling, M. A. (2000). Toward a general modular systems theory and its application to interfirm product modularity. *Academy of Management Review, 25*(2), 312–334.

Sharp, A. (1896). *Bicycles & tricycles. An elementary treatise on their design and construction with examples and tables*. London, UK: Longmans, Green, and Co.

Snow, D. C., Pisano, G., Corsi, E., & Urfalino, G. K. (2009). *Columbus tubing: Steel is real*. Case 9-609-042. Boston, MA: Harvard Business School Publishing.

Takeuchi, T. (1981). *The formation of the Japanese bicycle industry: A preliminary analysis of the infrastructure of the Japanese machine industry*. Tokyo, Japan: The United Nations University.

Takeuchi, T. (1991). The bicycle industry. In T. Takeuchi (Ed.), *The role of labour-intensive sectors in Japanese industrialization* (pp. 112–163). Tokyo, Japan: The United Nations University.

Tjong Tjin Tai, S., Veraart, F., & Davids, M. (2015). How the Netherlands became a bicycle nation: Users, firms and intermediaries, 1860–1940. *Business History, 57*(2), 257–289.

Trescott, M. M. (1976). The bicycle, a technical precursor of the automobile. *Business and Economic History, 5*, 51–75.

Ueda, T. (1981). *The development of the bicycle industry in Japan after World War II*. Tokyo, Japan: The United Nations University.

Ulrich, K. T. (1995). The role of product architecture in the manufacturing firm. *Research Policy, 24*, 419–440.

Vivanco, L. A. (2013). *Reconsidering the bicycle. An anthropological perspective on a new (old) thing*. New York, NY: Routledge.

Vota, G. (1954). *I Sessant'Anni del Touring Club Italiano 1894–1954*. Milan, Italy: Touring Club Italiano.

Wilson, D. G., & Papadopoulos, J. (2004). *Bicycling science* (3rd ed.). Cambridge, MA: The MIT Press.

Wilson, S. S. (1973). Bicycle technology. *Scientific American, 228*(3), 81–91.

Woodbury, P. (1960). The legend of Eli Whitney and interchangeable parts. *Technology and Culture, 1*(3), 235–253.

CHAPTER 2

Understanding the Market Through Bicycle Statistics

Abstract How many bicycles are manufactured each year in each country? How many of these are exported? How many bicycles are imported? How large is the domestic market for bicycles? How widespread is the bicycle in each country? The answers to these questions require data that can be used for informative and decision-making purposes. The chapter is a journey into the bicycle statistics available to emphasize current drawbacks and limitations. A selection of five statistics is presented through examples based on primary and secondary data drawn from the UK, Italy, the US, Canada, Japan and Taiwan.

Keywords Bicycle output · Exports · Imports · Apparent consumption · Bicycle ownership

The original version of this chapter was revised: The source line for Table 2.1 has been updated. The correction to this chapter is available at https://doi.org/10.1007/978-3-030-50563-9_5

C. Mari, *A Business History of the Bicycle Industry*,
https://doi.org/10.1007/978-3-030-50563-9_2

2.1 Why Bicycle Statistics Are Important and the Problems Associated with Them

Sound decisions generally stem from sound analysis based on data and information, which will reduce the level of uncertainty in making a decision. Successful managers are knowledgeable managers who have an understanding of the markets in which the organization competes. This is true for both a private profit-oriented firm and a public or a nonprofit organization. For instance, suppose that a marketing manager of a bicycle firm has to decide the new products to launch, or a mayor of a city has to choose whether to invest public money to build a bicycle infrastructure. In both cases, it is essential that the best possible solution is based on data available. Both marketing managers and city mayors are accountable to their stakeholders and using data and information in decision-making can lead to good outcomes, instead of relying on instinct and feelings that usually lead to bad outcomes. Bicycle statistics play a relevant role in providing a knowledge base to address issues regarding market opportunity, industry evolution and public policy to support the industry, city cycling, new road building, road maintenance and other decisions that can be improved if data are available. For example, statistics can facilitate measuring the number of potential people using the bicycle as a means of transportation or the potential number of cargo bicycles used to deliver goods. Bicycle statistics can highlight which kind of bicycle is preferred by cyclists and how the industry performs over time. Statistics can help to understand which countries are manufacturing, importing or exporting bicycles and components. Bicycle statistics can be used to frame a public policy intervention aimed at developing or improving the industry. Statistics can provide clues on the number of cyclists potentially interested in building a new road or can help to establish a linkage between the number of bicycles and road maintenance needs.

Bicycle statistics must possess certain characteristics if it is to be useful for decision-making. That is, statistics must be reliable, sufficient and comparable. Reliability refers to the degree to which statistics reflect reality and are accurate. Sufficient means that statistics must be complete so that data are not affected by any gaps. Comparability refers to the possibility that a sequence of data over time, or between one place and another, is measuring the same variable. A place can be a country, a geographical area or a bicycle firm. Bicycle statistics show serious problems with each of the three characteristics and it is not an exaggeration to state that data and information are plagued by unreliability, incompleteness and incomparability.

Moreover, bicycle statistics are affected by two further problems that make even more difficult to use them for decision-making or studying purposes. Firstly, bicycle data are not available and, secondly, if they are the access to them is not always guaranteed. Whoever attempted, at least once, to search for bicycle statistics, knows that it can prove a very challenging endeavour because of the almost complete lack of data. Practitioners, policymakers and scholars have to face the dilemma of understanding the bicycle industry with no or very few data. Unavailability of statistics is presumably due to the size of the industry that has been considered less significant than other industries with the consequence of preventing from gathering extensive data. Another possible explanation is that bicycles were considered jointly with other sets of goods, such as the means of transportation, within official statistics, and again the outcome was that no data specifically focused on bicycles were provided.

Even when data are available, it is not sure that they will be accessible. This is particularly true for proprietary statistics gathered by bicycle firms or trade associations. It is a very common practice for most of bicycle firms not to release their internal data. For instance, it is almost impossible to access a copy of the company annual report, except for a very small number of large firms, such as Accell Group (The Netherlands), Dorel (Canada), Fox Factory Holding Corp. (United States) and Shimano Inc. (Japan), which provide a digital version of their most recent annual reports. If a bicycle firm is too small for publishing an annual report, it could still release its basic data through other options less demanding than developing a complete annual report. Access to data remains particularly hard when someone is interested in knowing the number of bicycles manufactured by a firm. This piece of information is surrounded by a halo of secrecy that has become anachronistic over time and it cannot be explained through the usual recall of rivalry between the firms of the industry. According to the data available, the Accell Group is the only firm releasing the number of bicycles manufactured each year. Since 2004, its annual report includes such information (Accell Group 2005, 2006, 2007, 2008, 2009, 2010, 2011, 2012, 2013, 2014, 2015, 2016, 2017, 2018, 2019, 2020).

Bicycles statistics are usually provided by four primary sources in each country: office for national statistics, customs department, trade organization and bicycle firms. Each public office for statistics conduct periodically a census of industrial activity aimed at measuring variables such as output, employment, number of companies and company size. As already explained, very few data are available and it is difficult to build a long time series to understand how the bicycle industry evolved over time.

Customs departments are involved in gathering foreign trade statistics that record the physical movement of merchandise between countries. Export and import statistics are collected and compiled according to both national and international commodity classifications. For instance, the United Nations developed the Standard International Trade Classification (SITC) and the Harmonized Commodity Description and Coding System (also known as the HS) to allow comparability of international merchandise trade statistics; the European Union introduced its Combined Nomenclature (CN), which is based on the HS; and each country usually adds its own classification for further statistical needs. In Italy, imported or exported goods are classified using an 8-digit code number. This means that the level of disaggregation is higher than that of other classifications such as the HS that uses a 6-digit code number. The more digit there are in the code, the more precise the classification, and in turn the possibility of identifying the goods and gather relevant data increases as well. For example, Japanese customs agency classifies merchandise using a 9-digit code number. Export and import statistics record the quantity and the value of shipping goods. The former can be the number of units or the weight of merchandise, the latter is the value of transactions. Foreign trade statistics suffer from various limitations such as reporting errors (that is, mistakes or omissions) and timeliness (that is, import or export records not processed in time to be included in the current month's statistics may be carried over into a subsequent month's statistics). The timeliness problem requires a revision procedure usually on a monthly and annual base.

Trade organizations within the bicycle industry were established to collectively represent the manufacturers and protect their interests. In 1893, the Cycle Manufacturers Trade Protection Association was formed in England and renamed the Cycle & Motor Trades Association in 1900. Later, in 1910, it became the Cycle & Motor Cycle Manufacturers and Traders Union and in 1919 the British Cycle & Motor Cycle Manufacturers and Traders Union Ltd. (Millward 1999, p. 382). Italy, as mentioned in the previous chapter, formed its association of bicycle manufacturers in 1920 and called it ANCMA. In 2015, the Confederation of the European Bicycle Industry (CONEBI) was formed as a merger between the Association of the European Two-Wheeler Parts' and Accessories' Industry (COLIPED), established in 1960, and the Association of the European Bicycle Industry (COLIBI), established in 1973. Other countries formed similar organizations to combat the problems facing the industry as a whole. These associations usually provide some bicycle statistics, particularly those regarding the production of bicycles and components. They also compile foreign trade statistics using data gathered by the customs department. For instance, CONEBI releases a yearly short report describing the European bicycle industry. The report was issued for the first time in 2009 and was accessible free of charge until the 2017 edition, from the 2018 edition a payment is due. The bicycle statistics gathered by trade organizations share a common feature: the lack of an in-depth analysis of both industry and competitors in each country and worldwide.

Bicycle firms are the fourth source of bicycle statistics and, despite having some valuable data in their internal records, it is extremely difficult to access that information as already mentioned. This situation has not changed over time and it seems an entrenched practice within the industry all over the world.

The following sections of this chapter offer a sketch of bicycle statistics through examples of data available in different countries. The chapter is by no means a thorough description of all the statistics available within the industry. It is a starting point to scratch the surface of the topic. In approaching bicycle statistics, the first task is to understand what, if any, data exist, and what gaps and weaknesses affect those data. The chapter is focused on a limited selection of bicycle statistics that provide a fragmentary snapshot of the industry from a historical perspective. Five variables are presented as relevant for understanding a small piece of business history of the industry: the production of finished bicycles measured through the number of bicycles manufactured, the exports and imports of finished bicycles measured through the number of units involved in foreign trade, the apparent consumption measured through the number of bicycles potentially available for the domestic market and the bicycle ownership measured through the stock of bicycles in a country. All these variables are measured in quantity to make comparability between countries easier. Some bicycle statistics, particularly those regarding exports and imports of bicycles and components, are also measured in value. This chapter does not include any statistics measured in value to prevent the problem associated with comparing different currencies and their exchange rate over time.

2.2 Bicycle Production Statistics

This section examines data regarding the output of the bicycle industry as a whole in six countries, presented in the following order: the UK, Italy, the US, Canada, Japan and Taiwan. As already mentioned, the statistics available do not allow to draw a complete picture of the industry in those countries, nevertheless they can help to acquire a preliminary knowledge of the size of bicycle production.

Statistics for UK are based on two secondary sources (Millward 1999, pp. 160, 279–280; Rosen 2002, pp. 73, 120) that compiled data from various primary sources. The time series built on both sources covers the years from 1876 to 1995, however many data are missing and it is not possible to fill in the gap. A thorough interpretation of these data requires an extensive study that is beyond the scope of this chapter. It is clear from the chart shown in Fig. 2.1 that UK bicycle industry had a significant growth during the 1930s and the 1950s. Its production began to decrease in the mid-1970s and the size of its output reached a pick of about 3.5 million units in the 1950s, and was over 1 million units in the 1990s.

Further data are from the internal records of the most important British firm: Raleigh Cycle Company. The time series shows the production of bicycles from 1896 to 1959 at Raleigh (Rosen 2002, pp. 52–53). There are two missing data (1906 and 1958) and all the years ending in August. The graph (Fig. 2.2) highlights that the contribution of Raleigh to bicycle production of UK industry was fundamental. The existence of such statistics corroborates the hypothesis that some bicycle firms do collect their own data, even though they are not easily released.

Bicycle production statistics in Italy cover the 1950–2019 time frame. Before 1950 very few data are available from scattered sources. An estimate of bicycle output between 1907 and 1914 shows that Italian industry manufactured an average of 146,000 finished bicycles, ranging from 98,062 in 1907 to 221,612 in 1910 (Piloni 1982, p. 49). The time series provided by the trade organization ANCMA (2019, 2020) is plotted in Fig. 2.3 and reveals a first period, from 1950 to 1958, characterized by steady bicycle production of approximately 400,000 pieces. In the subsequent period, from 1959 to 1965, bicycle production increased 2.5 times and reached approximately 1,000,000 pieces. From 1966 to 1978 and from 1979 to 1989, bicycle production showed a further growth of 100%, reaching 2,000,000 pieces and 3,000,000 pieces, respectively. The years from 1990 to 1994 are the last growth trend in the complete time series. The peak, of 5,800,000 bicycles, is observed in 1994. A significant decline whereby bicycle production is reduced approximately by 60% begins in 1995 and lasts until 2002. Bicycle production fluctuates from 2002 to 2019 and then upward to approximately 2,600,000 pieces.

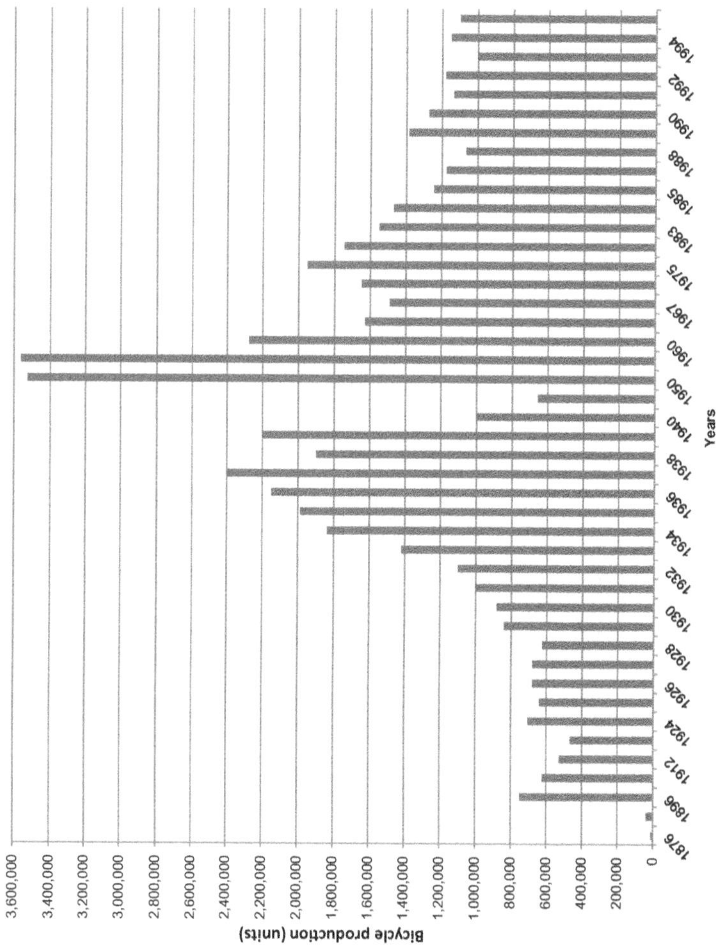

Fig. 2.1 British bicycle production 1876–1995

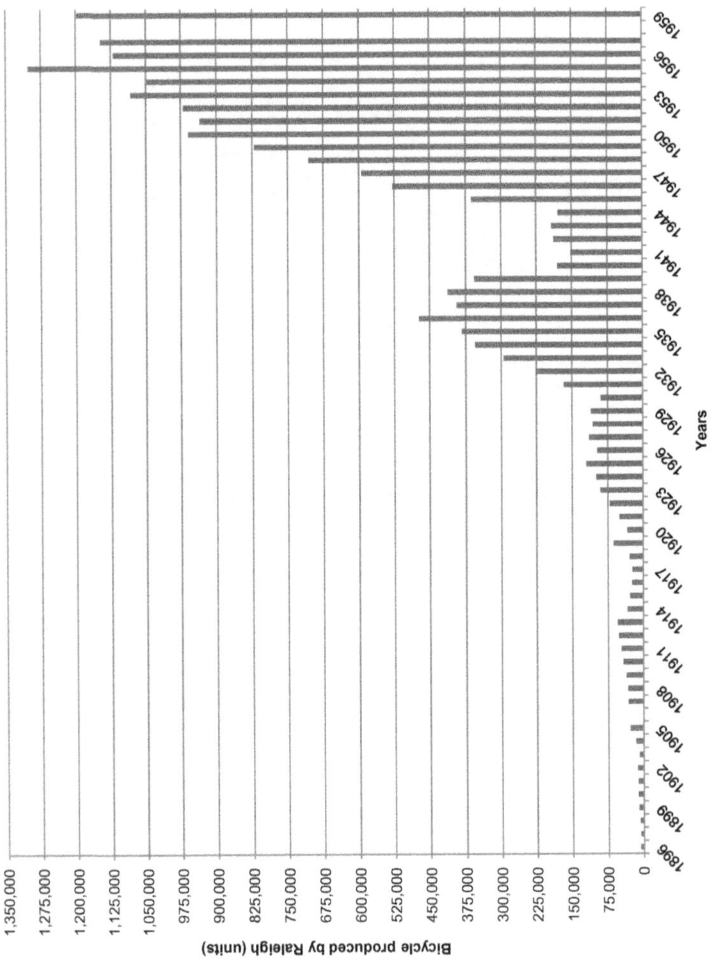

Fig. 2.2 Bicycle production by Raleigh 1896–1959

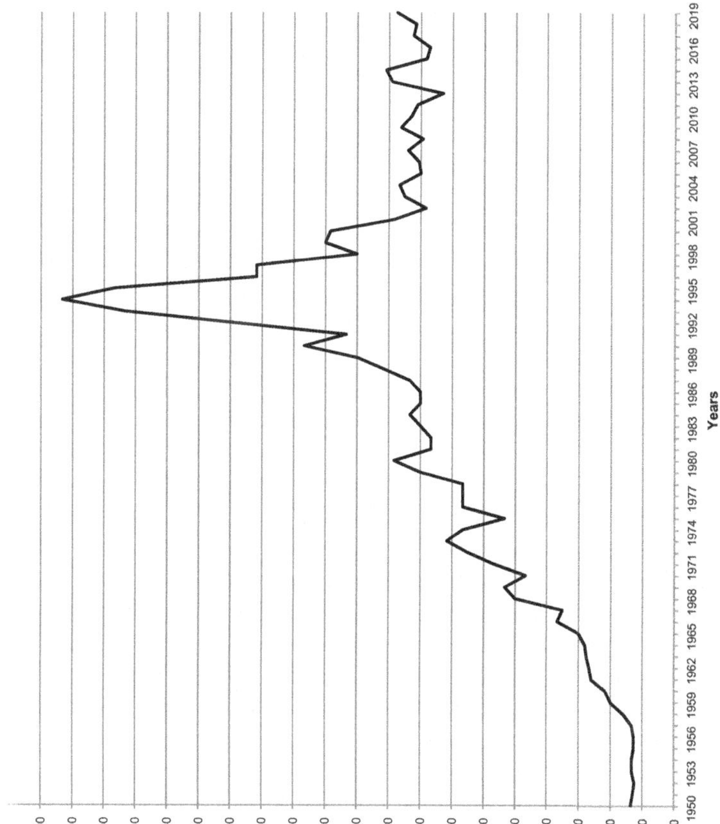

Fig. 2.3 Italian bicycle production 1950–2019

The statistics from ANCMA show two main limitations. Firstly, the data represent an estimate of the domestic production of bicycles, not actual production. Secondly, the process of estimation is based on the assumption that one bicycle frame is equivalent to one bicycle. ANCMA makes an estimate of the number of frames, both manufactured in Italy and imported, that becomes a proxy for the number of bicycles produced every year as explained by ANCMA's director of bicycle industry (Nigrelli 2018). According to ANCMA, the bicycle production estimate has a margin of error of plus or minus 50,000 bicycles. Although the time series is 69 years long, it seems more reasonable to state that such a margin of error applies to the recent years, presumably since the 2000s. Moreover, it is not clear how the number of bicycle frames is estimated, particularly the domestic production of frames. The number of imported bicycle frames is not an estimate, as such data are available through the official statistics provided ex post by the Italian Customs Agency. A further issue stemming from the process of estimation is that estimation methods might have been changed over time. If more than one method of estimation was used, a comparability issue has to be considered, as it is necessary to understand if two different methods were employed to measure the same variable.

Statistics for the United States of America are drawn from two secondary sources (Epperson 2001, 2012; Chu and Li 1997, p. 60) that provide an initial understanding of bicycle output in that country. The data, covering the early years of US bicycle industry from 1878 to 1914, clearly show the so-called bicycle boom during the second half of the 1890s when production reached its peak of approximately 1,300,000 units (Fig. 2.4). Epperson's contribution is one of the very few studies specifically devoted to the topic of bicycle statistics, and it offers a valuable analysis of the US context.

The other source compiles data from further secondary sources and it is focused on a more contemporary situation regarding the years from 1966 to 1991. The chart in Fig. 2.5 highlights the sharp increase during the first half of the 1970s when bicycle output increased to over 10 million units. The average yearly bicycle production during this time frame was approximately 6,400,000 pieces.

There are very few sources regarding bicycle statistics in Canada and one of these provides a time series from 1920 to 1959 (Babaian 1998, p. 105) compiled using various primary data. The graph of bicycle production (Fig. 2.6) shows two peaks during the second half of both

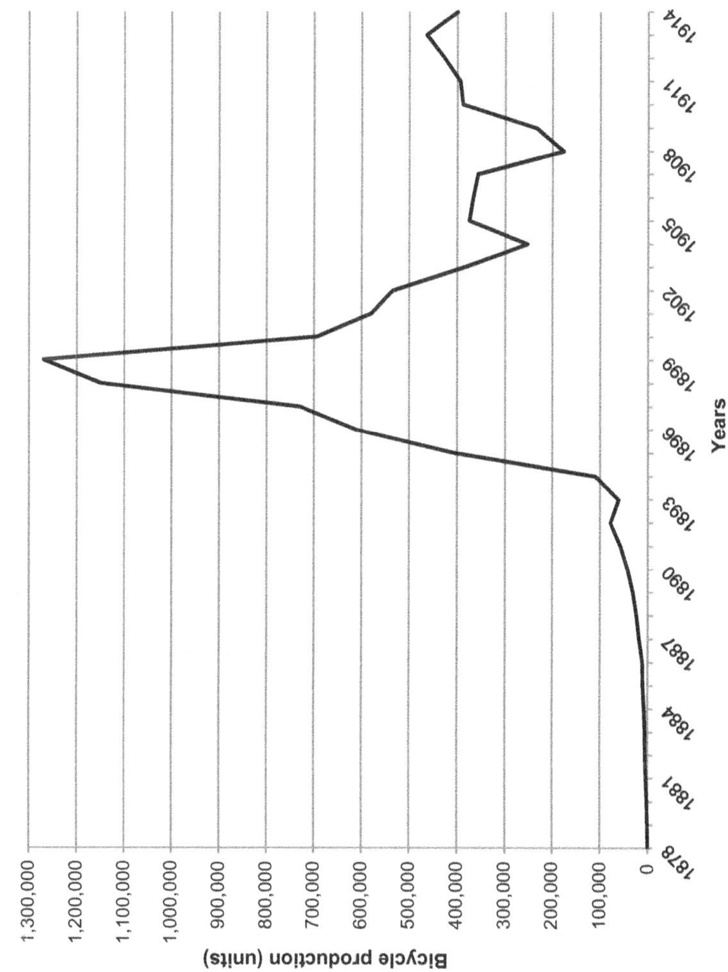

Fig. 2.4 US bicycle production 1878–1914

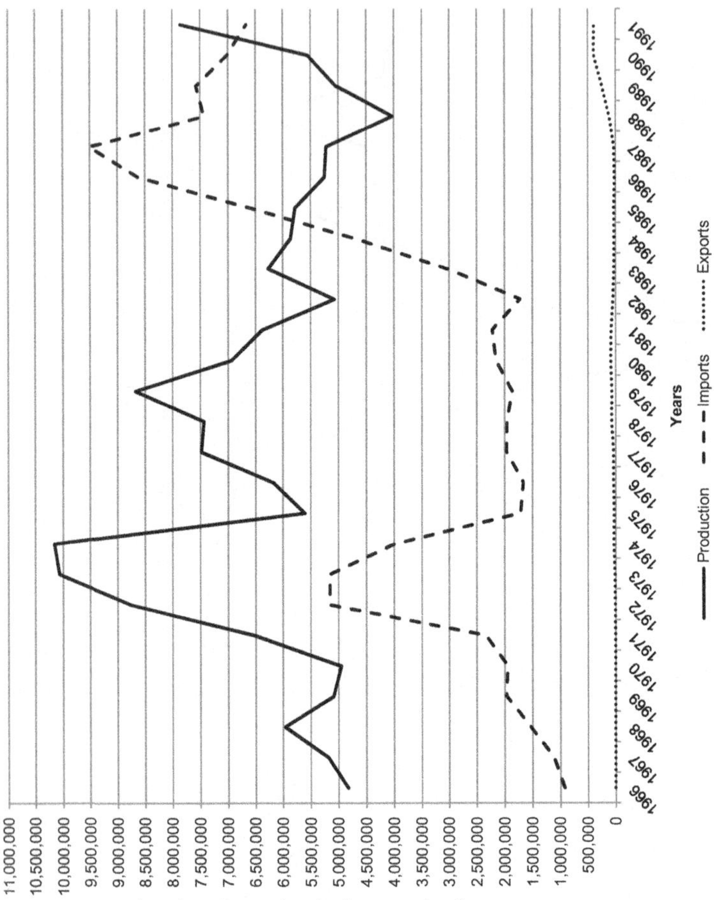

Fig. 2.5 US bicycle statistics 1966–1991

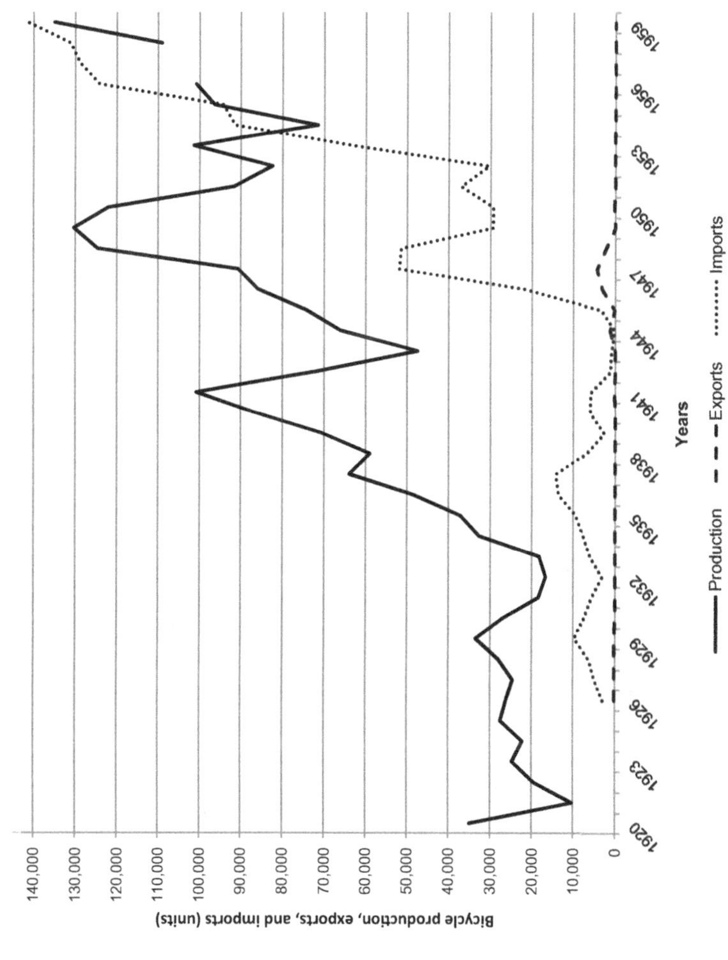

Fig. 2.6 Canadian bicycle statistics 1920–1959

the 1930s and 1940s. One year is missing (that is 1957) and the average yearly output was approximately 62,000 units.

Bicycle production statistics in Japan are available for a long time series, even though there are some gaps arising from the different sources examined (Takeuchi 1991, p. 137; Ueda 1981, p. 45; Kotha and Fried 1993, p. 13; Japan Bicycle Promotion Institute 2019, p. 5). Takeuchi studies the formation and the development of the bicycle industry until the 1930s, using the Ministry of Commerce and Industry's statistics from 1929 to 1938. Ueda examines the history of the post-war Japanese bicycle industry, focusing on the 1950s and 1960s, and provides output data from 1923 to 1978 based on various primary sources. The case study developed by Kotha & Fried includes bicycle production data from 1982 to 1991, gathered by the Japan Bicycle Manufacturer's Association. The Japan Bicycle Promotion Institute compiles data, covering the 2004–2018 time frame, based on the Ministry of Economy, Trade and Industry (METI) Current Production Statistics. A limitation of these statistics is the gap within the time series. The years from 1979 to 1981 and from 1992 to 2003 are missing. The chart in Fig. 2.7 shows the peak of production during the first half of the 1970s when most countries experienced the bicycle boom, and the stabilization of bicycle output to around 7 million units in the 1980s. Current data, since 2004, emphasize the significant decrease of bicycle production from approximately 2,454,000 pieces in 2004 to 850,000 pieces in 2018.

There are both primary and secondary sources of bicycle statistics for a preliminary understanding of the Taiwanese industry. The former is the Ministry of Economic Affairs of Taiwan (2020) that provides a time series from 1981 to 2019, easily accessible through its website in English language. The latter is a study that provides bicycle output data from 1968 to 1992 using an estimate method based on export statistics and domestic sales (Chu and Li 1996, 1997). The rationale is that the export data, collected by the customs office, have a broader coverage that makes them more reliable, whereas the industrial production data have a smaller coverage and firms routinely misrepresent their sale data, presumably for tax purposes (Chu and Li 1997, p. 70). According to this study, reliable statistics became available only in the late 1970s. The graph of bicycle output in Fig. 2.8 is based on secondary data for the period 1968–1980 and primary data from 1981 through 2019. The chart shows the huge increase during the 1970s and 1980s when the production jumped from 394,000 units in 1971 to approximately 10,738,000 units in 1987. Later,

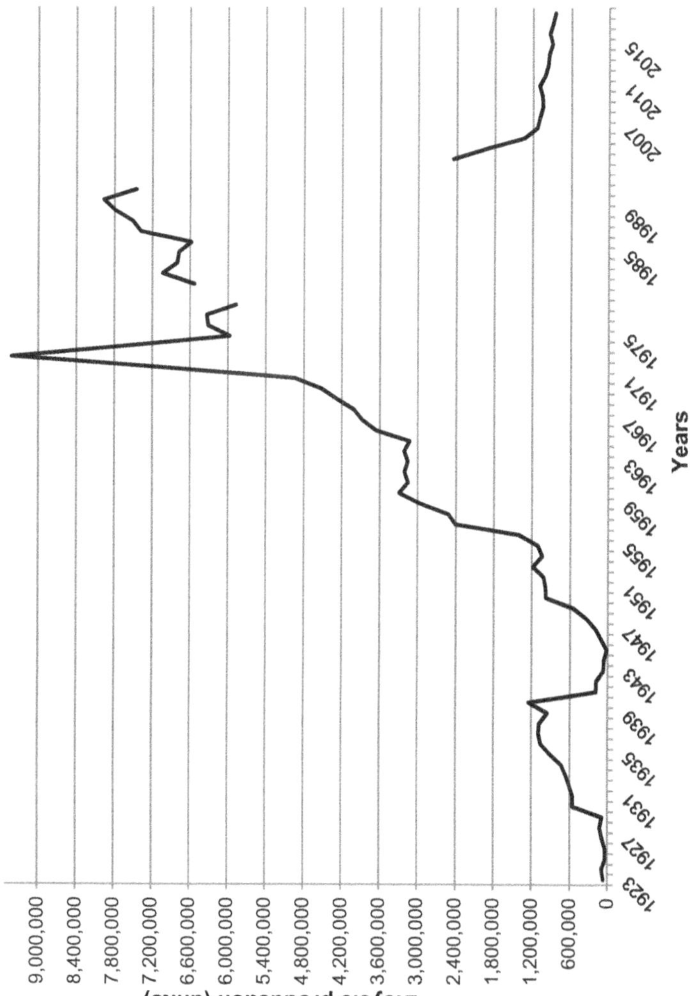

Fig. 2.7 Japanese bicycle production 1923–2018

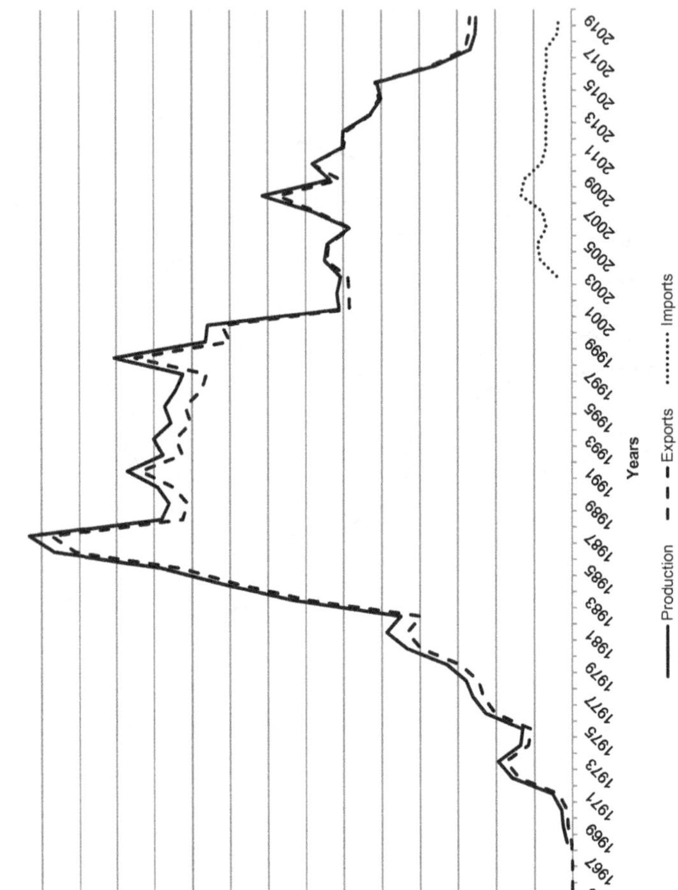

Fig. 2.8 Taiwanese bicycle statistics 1965–2019

bicycle output stabilized around 8 million pieces until 2000. Since the 2000s, the size of bicycle production significantly decreases to reach the lowest level of approximately 1,880,000 units in 2019. Presumably, the explanation of such a situation is the choice made by large bicycle firms, such as Giant and Merida, to move in part their production capacity to countries where the cost of labour is lower than Taiwan.

2.3 Bicycle Export and Import Statistics

This section analyses export and import data of the bicycle industry as a whole and reiterates the same organization of the previous section presenting a short discussion of six countries: the UK, Italy, the US, Canada, Japan and Taiwan.

The time series of British exports range from 1907 to 1939 and is incomplete as many years are missing, particularly those between 1908 and 1923 (Millward 1999, p. 278). According to these data, UK was an exporting country and played a key role in influencing the bicycle industry in other geographical areas, as explained in the previous chapter. During the 1920s and the 1930s the average yearly exports increased from approximately 255,000 units to 400,000 units (Fig. 2.9).

Bicycle import data are based on two time series, from different sources (Millward 1999, p. 279; Rosen 2002, p. 120), which provide a wider picture than the export statistics. The first set of data covers the 1902–1939 time frame and the second includes some years within the 1967–1992 range, showing many gaps. Despite some cautions that must be kept in mind when interpreting data outside their context, it is plausible to suggest that until the 1930s the United Kingdom imported very few bicycles, with the exception of 1902 that is difficult to explain (Fig. 2.10a). The situation completely changed since 1975 when bicycle imports began to climb and reached a yearly average of approximately 1,500,000 units (Fig. 2.10b).

Italy adopted an import-substitution industrialization model as discussed in the previous chapter and foreign trade statistics support this argument. Two time series are available from a secondary and a primary source. The former is a study (Piloni 1982, pp. 27–28) providing data covering the birth and early development of the industry from 1878 to 1914, with one year missing (that is 1895). The latter is the database of the Italian office for national statistics, called Istituto Nazionale di Statistica (ISTAT), which compiles data drawn from the customs agency

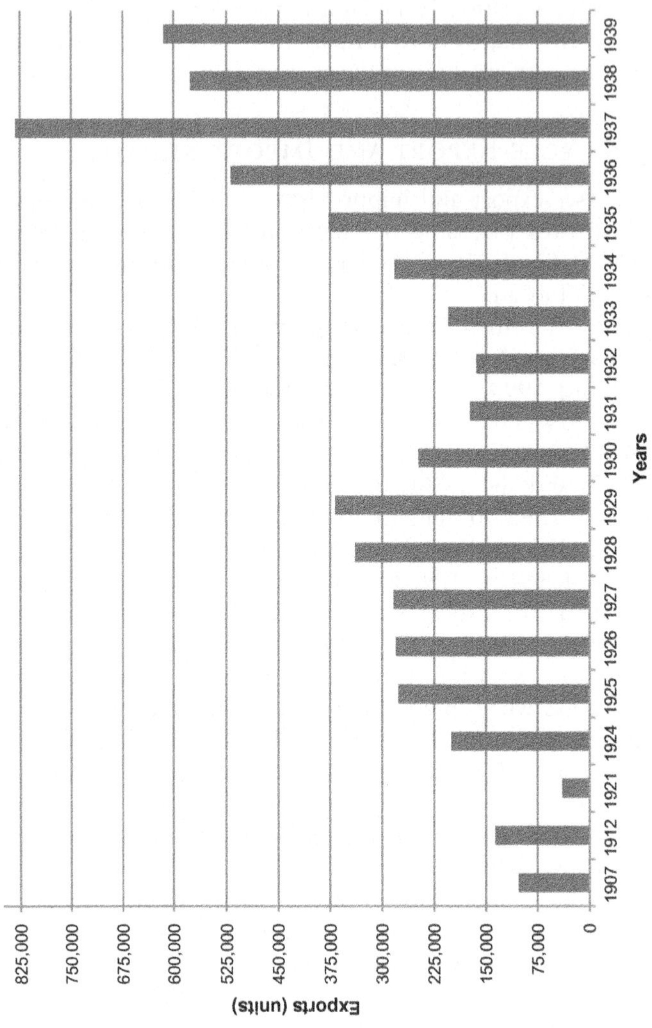

Fig. 2.9 British bicycle exports 1907–1939

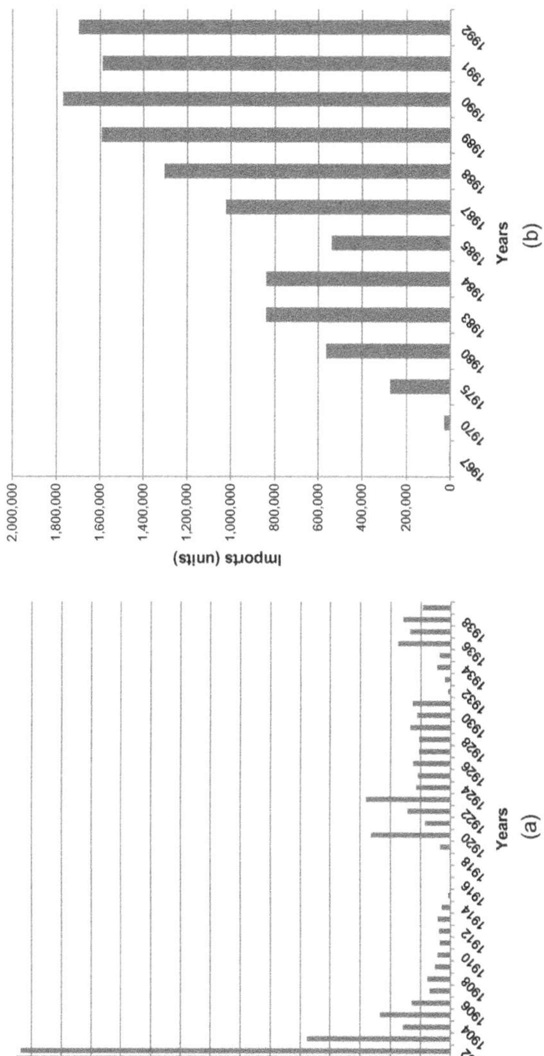

Fig. 2.10 British bicycle imports 1902–1992 **a** 1902–1939 and **b** 1967–1992

records. This data set includes a time series from 1994 to 2019 for finished bicycles and from 1991 to 2019 for bicycle frames (Istituto Nazionale di Statistica 2020). Before the 1990s it is not possible to identify both bicycles and bicycle frames as they were combined with other goods, preventing any deeper analysis. This is the result of the changes that, repeatedly over time, affect the Combined Nomenclature, particularly the level of data aggregation that, in turn, impacts on the possibility of isolating bicycles form other goods. Figure 2.11 is the chart of the first time series showing that bicycle imports were a significant source for the Italian market until the end of the 1890s and during the 1910s, even though the nascent industry began to compensate with exports.

The second time series, focused on more contemporary data, shows a declining trend in bicycle exports since 1994 and a stabilization around to a yearly average of 1,536,000 units (Fig. 2.12). The import of bicycles is characterized by a growth trend between 1994 and 2005, when the number of imported bicycles increased tenfold, reaching approximately 811,000 pieces in 2005. From 2006 to 2017, the import of bicycles fluctuated upward and downward around approximately 675,000 pieces. Later, imports decreased significantly in 2018 and indicated a recovery in

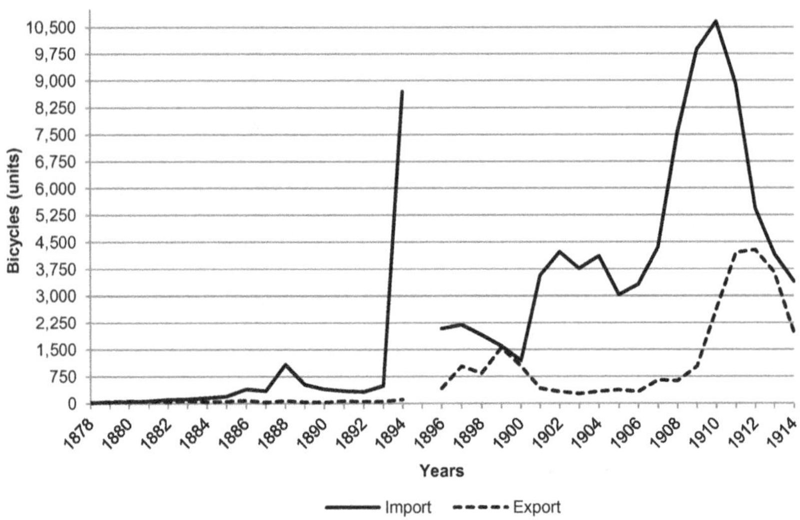

Fig. 2.11 Italian bicycle exports and imports 1878–1914

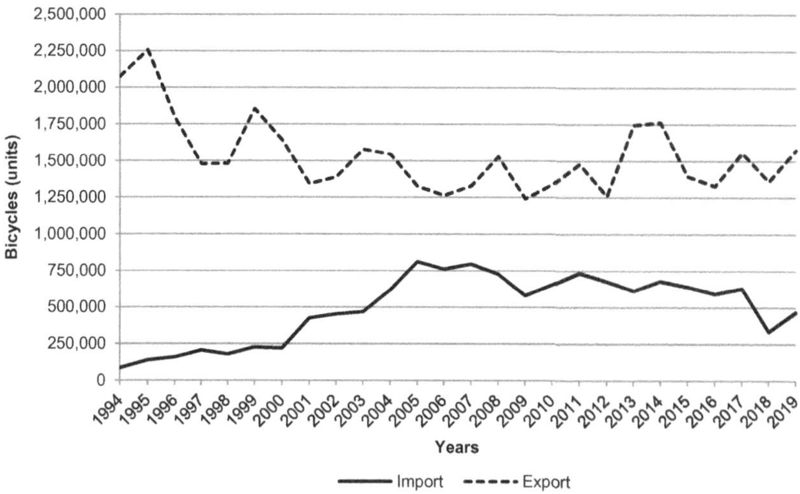

Fig. 2.12 Italian bicycle exports and imports 1994–2019

2019. This last year data are still provisional and subject to change when the final revision from ISTAT will be available.

As discussed in the previous chapter, Italian bicycle firms have almost completely set frame fabrication aside and this change is clearly visible through foreign trade statistics. The export of Italian bicycle frames was significant between 1991 and 1999 (Fig. 2.13). There was a more than fivefold increase, and the figure eventually reached 1,268,000 pieces. From 2000 to 2004, however, there was a dramatic decrease that reduced frame exports by approximately 83%. Since 2005, the yearly average number of exported bicycle frames was approximately 197,000 pieces. The import of bicycle frames shows an almost ninefold increase from 1991 to 2002, eventually reaching 2,340,000 pieces. The number of imported frames rose sharply from 2003 to 2004 and reached a peak of 4,051,000 pieces. From 2005, there was a decrease characterized by upward and downward fluctuations, and the yearly average number of bicycle frames was approximately 2,890,000 units. The last year is a provisional data, waiting for the usual revision due to the timeliness problem, and it shows a sharp drop in the number of bicycle frame imported. Despite the 2019 data, the figures about bicycle frames indicate that

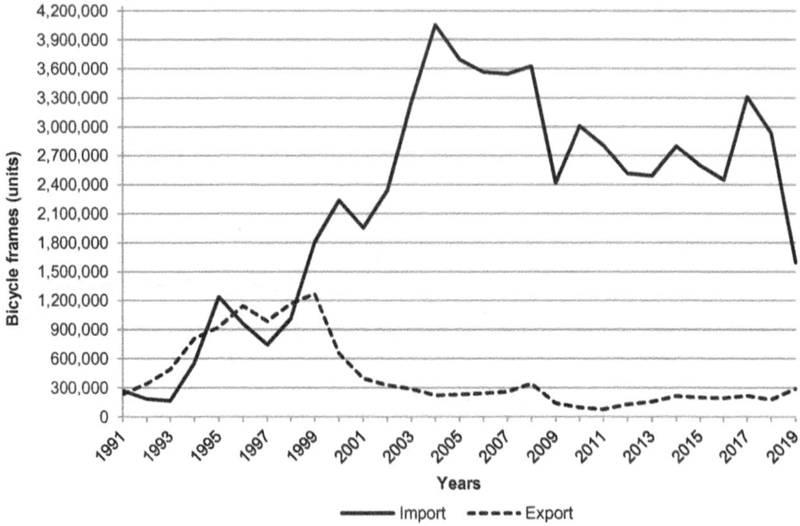

Fig. 2.13 Italian bicycle frame exports and imports 1991–2019

Italian bicycle companies are progressively replacing the manufacturing of frames with the import of products, presumably from Asia.

The export and import statistics of finished bicycle by the US industry is plotted in Fig. 2.5 where a 26-year time series, already examined in the previous section, shows that during the 1966–1991 time frame exports were almost negligible, except at the end of the 1980s and the beginning of the 1990s. Instead, bicycle imports played a key role into the domestic market, particularly during the first half of the 1970s and most of the 1980s until 1987 when a peak of approximately 9,500,000 units was reached.

A similar situation happened in Canada, during the 1926–1959 time frame (Fig. 2.6), where exports were negligible as well, and bicycle imports served the domestic market adding a significant number of units, particularly since the second half of the 1930s and after the end of the World War II.

The sources used for Japan's foreign trade statistics are the same as those already examined to discuss bicycle production. Export data are based on three time series. The first covering the 1930–1978 time frame, with some gaps (that is the years 1931–1932 are missing); the second from 1982 through 1991; and the third from 2001 until 2018. Figure 2.14 shows the graph of bicycle exports, which became a notable achievement for the industry since the end of the 1950s until 1974, with a peak of 1,546,000 units in 1972. Later, there were downward and upward fluctuations for about 10 years, followed by a sudden decrease until 1991, when the export of bicycles reached 203,000 units. The 2000s saw a sequence of 15-years increase until 2015, with approximately 3,558,000 bicycles exported. Afterwards, the exports reversed direction and began to fall.

The import of bicycles in Japan can be broken down into three distinct phases based on the time series available. The first phase from the inception of the industry through 1972 (Fig. 2.15a) is another example of the import-substitution industrialization model. Imports progressively decline as local production of bicycles increases. There are some discrepancies and inconsistencies between data provided by Takeuchi (1991) and Ueda (1981) and further sources were used to address the problem. The sources are the annual statistics of foreign trade from The Department of Finance

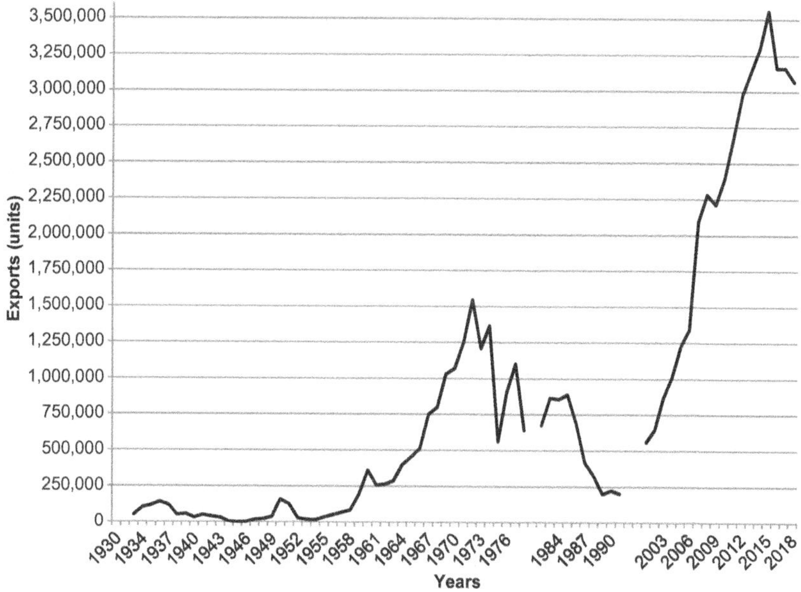

Fig. 2.14 Japanese bicycle exports 1930–2018

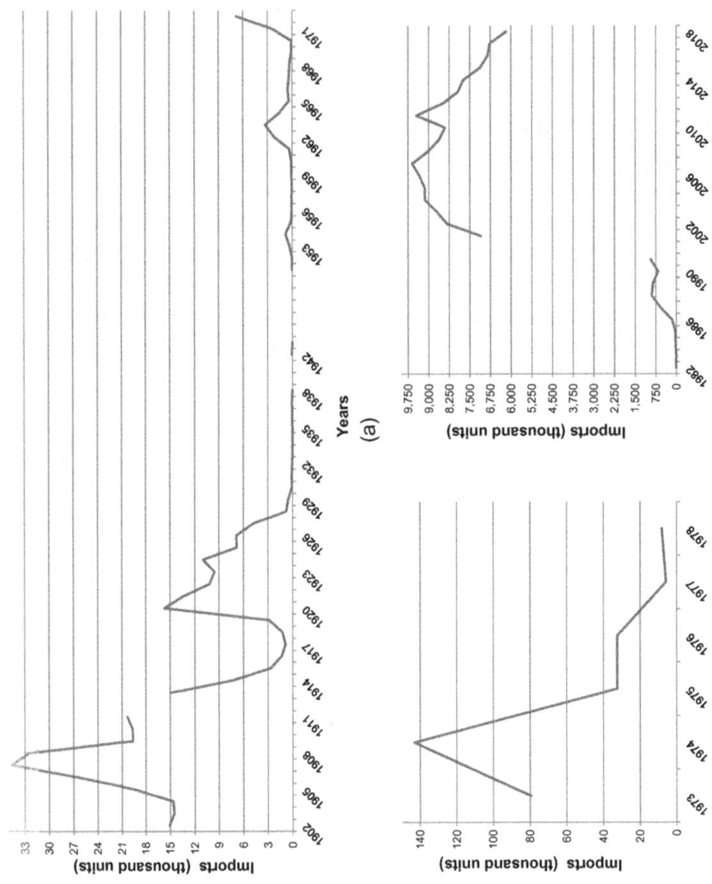

Fig. 2.15 Japanese bicycle imports 1902–2018 **a** 1902–1972, **b** 1973–1978, and **c** 1982–2018

(n.d.a, b) and the overview of the bicycle industry developed by the Japan Association of Bicycle Manufacturers (1979). During the second phase, from 1973 to 1978, imports reached the highest peak to over 143,000 units in 1974 (Fig. 2.15b). The last phase, from 1982 through 2018, can be divided into sub-time periods. The first, covering the 1982–1991 time frame, saw a significant growth of imports to 940,000 pieces in 1991 (Fig. 2.15c). The second period, from 2001 through 2018, marked a steady increase of imports with a yearly average of approximately 8,800,000 units until 2011. Afterwards, bicycle imports began to decrease to approximately 6,182,000 units in 2018.

The export data of Taiwan are based on the same sources already used for bicycle production statistics. Secondary data cover the 1965–1980 time frame and primary data are from 1981 until 2019. Foreign trade statistics of the Taiwanese bicycle industry highlight that bicycle export is a fundamental activity for local firms as their output is almost completely sold to other countries. The graph of bicycle export (Fig. 2.8) shows that the time series of both production and exports are fully overlapped. In some years the number of exported bicycles exceeds that of production, presumably the time series has not been revised yet. There are no import data by the Ministry of Economic Affairs of Taiwan. Import statistics are available through the database of Customs Administration that provides a time series from 2003 to 2019 (Customs Administration of Taiwan 2020). Imports of finished bicycles reached a peak of approximately one million units in 2008 and then began to decrease to approximately 252,000 units in 2019 (Fig. 2.8). The average yearly imports were approximately 546,000 units during this period of time.

2.4 Apparent Consumption Statistics

It is a very common practice in the bicycle industry to use export and import data to create a further statistics to understand the size of domestic market. This statistics is called apparent consumption and is considered a proxy for domestic sales of bicycles. It is derived residually as the difference between bicycle production and net exports, which in turn is the algebraic sum of import and export data. The use of apparent consumption is justified as the only way to grasp bicycle unit sales of a specific country in a specific year. Although such a practice is understandable, it is flawed conceptually and methodologically. The concept of bicycle unit sales is different from that of apparent consumption. The former is the number of bicycles actually sold, while the latter combines the number of bicycles manufactured, usually obtained through an estimation process, and the number of bicycles actually imported and exported, usually subject to a long revision process. Apparent consumption is also problematic from a methodological perspective, as it does not account for inventory at the retail and wholesale levels. This means that it is not possible to know how many bicycles remain unsold. Bicycle production data provide an estimate of what was manufactured but do not determine the actual number of bicycles sold. Even though the net exports are based on actual data, they do not necessarily indicate that an imported or exported bicycle was also sold; it could still be unsold at some point within the distribution channels. The interpretation of apparent consumption requires caution because of the limitations highlighted earlier and the composite nature of such a variable. Moreover, the use of apparent consumption seems more appropriate when the focus of the analysis is understanding the status of the domestic market rather than the status of industry performance.

The time series of bicycle production, exports and imports examined in previous sections do not allow to compute the apparent consumption statistics for each country due to many missing data. Therefore, the following example is based on a long time series of 26 years describing the contemporary Italian bicycle market. Figure 2.16 shows the apparent consumption from 1994 to 2019. The domestic market decreased by approximately 56% from 1994 to 1999, and it fluctuated in subsequent years, reaching a yearly average of approximately 1,665,000 bicycles. Apparent consumption cannot provide enough clues to evaluate the market situation of a geographical area. It is a rough estimate that needs further information to understand how well or bad that bicycle market is performing.

2.5 Bicycle Ownership Statistics

A further statistics that might shed light on the bicycle industry is the stock of bicycles available in a country or, as it is usually called, bicycle ownership. This statistics provides a preliminary knowledge about how widespread is the bicycle within the population of a country. It is an aggregate measure that tells something about the size of bicycle adoption by a specific population, which can be the inhabitants of a country, a region, a city, or a town. Bicycle ownership suffers from the same problems as those

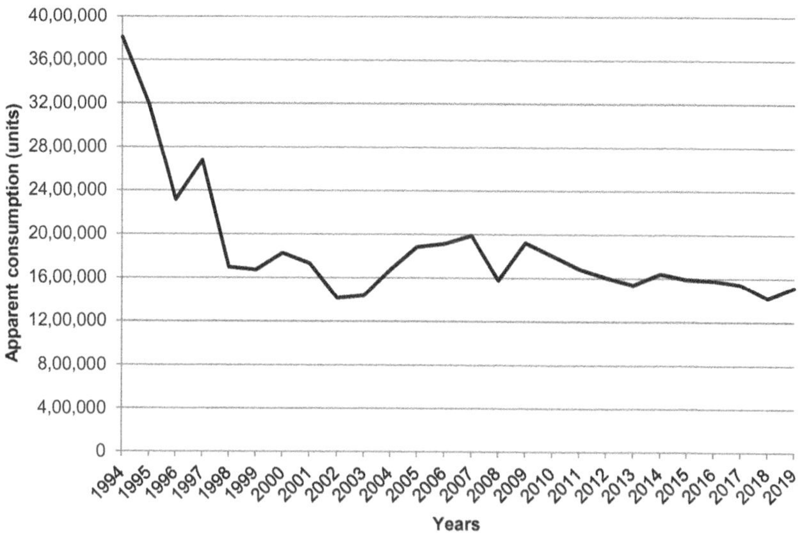

Fig. 2.16 Italian apparent consumption 1994–2019

already referred to as other bicycle statistics. It is very difficult to find bicycle ownership data available and, if data exist, they are usually unreliable, incomplete and incomparable. This section includes two examples of bicycle ownership statistics from Italy and Japan. The other countries, such as the UK, US, Canada and Taiwan, have no or very limited data. The Italian case (Mari 2018) offers an in-depth analysis of the topic and highlights most of the problems associated with this statistics.

Statistics about bicycle ownership in Italy are drawn primarily from magazines published by the Touring Club Ciclistico Italiano (TCCI), a national organization of cyclists focused upon tourism founded in Milan in 1894. Three relevant magazines were reviewed: *Rivista Mensile del T.C.I.* (published from 1895 to 1920), *Le Vie d'Italia* (published from 1917 to 1943 and from 1946 to 1967), and *Le Strade* (published from 1919 to 1943 and from 1946 to 1970). The TCCI used to compile a report of bicycle ownership that was published in one of the organization's magazines. Raw data were drawn from two sources: bicycle registration plates and membership reports. The first source was based on data gathered by the Ministry of Finance, and it was the prevailing channel used to understand how bicycle ownership evolved over time in the country, whereas the second source was not very frequent, presumably due to practical difficulties and cost issues. Bicycle registration was introduced for taxation purposes in 1897, and any bicycle had to have its own plate, attached to the bicycle frame, showing that the tax was paid. Such registration was a very controversial initiative that aroused the opposition of cyclists and their advocates, such as the TCCI. The tax was reduced in 1910 and then abolished in 1927. It was reintroduced in 1931, and its final abolishment was announced in 1938 (with implementation beginning in 1939). Table 2.1 shows the data available drawn from varied and scattered sources. The figures cover the time period from 1895 to 1959. It is even more difficult to find further data on bicycle ownership after the 1950s. Table 2.1 highlights some gaps in the sequence that makes the time series incomplete and more difficult to interpret. The number of bicycles increased approximately tenfold from 1895 to 1905. There was approximately one bicycle for every 150 people in 1901 and one bicycle for every 60 people in 1911. The adoption of bicycles greatly increased until the 1950s. In 1921 there was one bicycle for every 23 people and in 1936 one bicycle for every 11 people. After World War II, there was one bicycle for every 6 people in 1951 and one bicycle for every 5 people in 1959.

Data usually were available if the bicycle registration tax was due, as the Ministry of Finance created its own statistics for taxation purposes. It was more difficult to obtain data on bicycle ownership when the tax was abolished, as happened in some years. In addition to the problem of accessibility, the use of data on the bicycle registration tax for statistical analysis has some drawbacks. Firstly, tax evasion was a relevant issue, and many sources in Table 2.1 claim that figures usually underestimate the true number of bicycles. There are not any estimates of the size of tax evasion, but the perception is that the problem had a significant impact on the reliability of the statistics. Secondly, there was a tax exemption for some kind of bicycles, such as military and police bicycles; consequently, figures do not include those bicycles. It is not possible to know how many bicycles were exempted, but the military and police still used bicycles as a means of transportation until the 1940s. Thirdly, the figures should match the number of bicycles, but this is not necessarily true. Some sources claim that a better interpretation is the number of registration plates or the number of cyclists. This means that some cyclists, who owned more than one bicycle, attempted to pay the registration tax just once even though they were required to pay it for each bicycle. They simply moved the

Table 2.1 Italian bicycle ownership 1895–1959

Year	Bicycle ownership	Source	Bicycle ownership	Source	Bicycle ownership	Source	Bicycle ownership	Source	Bicycle ownership	Source	Year
1895	30,000	(a)									
1898			185,000	(t)							
1899	109,019	(b), (c)	200,000	(t)			111,027	(y)			1898-1899
1900	124,861	(c)	215,000	(t)			128,245	(y)	126,080	(z)	1899-1900
1901	142,918	(c)	221,000	(t)			141,358	(z)			1900-1901
1902	174,507	(c)	230,000	(t)							
1903	200,887	(d)	242,000	(t)							
1904			295,000	(t)			239,691	(aa)			1903-1904
1905			343,000	(t)							
1906			368,000	(t)							
1907			412,000	(t)			368,181	(bb)			1906-1907
1908			475,000	(t)							
1909			504,000	(t)							
1910			605,000	(t)			606,195	(cc)			1909-1910
1911							930,651	(cc)			1910-1911
1912							996,182	(cc)			1911-1912
1913							1,109,354	(cc)			1912-1913
1914	1,250,701	(e)									
1915	1,276,476	(e)									
1916	1,070,573	(e)									
1917	1,055,419	(e)									
1918	1,067,069	(e)									
1919	1,363,936	(e)									
1920	1,603,569	(e)									
1921	1,685,533	(e)	1,849,272	(u)							
1922	1,849,272	(e)									
1923	2,039,161	(e)									
1924	2,224,025	(e)	2,223,995	(h)	2,264,105	(u)					
1925	2,549,718	(f), (g), (h), (i)									
1926	2,896,523	(i)									
1927	3,275,000	(j)									
1928	3,670,000	(j)									
1929	4,070,000	(j)									
1930	4,480,000	(j)									
1932	3,500,000	(k)									
1933	3,476,721	(l), (w)	3,465,791	(v)			3,443,767	(x)			
1934	3,655,460	(l)	3,650,050	(v)	3,554,940	(w)	3,637,588				
1935	3,992,076	(l)					3,982,851				
1936	4,019,509	(m)					4,047,640				
1937	4,493,124	(n)					4,504,861				
1938	4,935,019	(o)					4,954,117				
1939	6,000,000	(p)									
1940	4,000,000	(q)									
1941	5,000,000	(q)									
1948	8,000,000	(r)									
1949	8,000,000	(r)									
1950	8,000,000	(r)									
1951	8,000,000	(r)									
1952	8,000,000	(r)									
1953	8,000,000	(r)									
1954	7,000,000	(r)									
1955	7,000,000	(r)									
1959	10,870,000	(s)									

Source (a) Johnson (1896); (b) Bertarelli (1900); (c) Anonymous (1903); (d) Anonymous (1904); (e) Ceriani (1926); (f) Anonymous (1926); (g) Spaventa Filippi (1927); (h) Vandone (1927a); (i) Vandone (1927b); (j) Vandone (1930); (k) Vandone (1934); (l) Anonymous (1936); (m) Anonymous (1937); (n) Anonymous (1938); (o) Anonymous (1939); (p) ANCMA (1953); (q) Anonymous (1942); (r) Roghi (1956); (s) Luzzatto Fegiz (1960); (t) Roseo (1912); (u) Anonymous (1924); (v) Vandone (1935); (w) Gazzaniga (1935); (x) Biffi (1941); (y) Bianchi (1901); (z) Brentari (1902); (aa) Anonymous (1905); (bb) Bianchi (1908); (cc) Bertarelli (1915) plate from one bicycle to another. Available data do not make it possible know the average number of bicycles owned by each cyclist, but it is reasonable to state that the majority of Italian families had more than one bicycle, as it was the most affordable means of transportation until the 1940s. Fourthly, bicycle registration statistics were determined for taxation purposes and very seldom distinguished among bicycles, tandems, tricycles, quadricycles and motorized bicycles. Figures usually include all these vehicles, and it is not possible to know the quantity for each category. It is plausible to state that bicycles were the largest group within those vehicles. Fifthly, the Ministry of Finance used a fiscal year that was different from the calendar year, and statistics follow the former in some cases, whereas in other cases, they follow the latter. The comparability of the time series is jeopardized, as it is not always clear on which year (fiscal or calendar) the data available are based.

Table 2.1 is organized to emphasize the discrepancies and inconsistencies arising from the different sources quoted below the table. There are five columns each for *Bicycle ownership* and for *Source*. For each year, the reader can see the available figures, the alternative figures (when they exist) and the sources reported in the reference section of the chapter. There are some data in the upper-right corner of Table 2.1 that the sources reported according to fiscal year (included in the last column of the table). Such a year usually began on July 1 and ended on June 30 of the next year (for example, from July 1, 1898, to June 30, 1899). It is clear from Table 2.1 that bicycle statistics often contradict each other and, in many cases, are rough estimates that require caution in interpretation. A possible explanation of discrepancies and inconsistencies, besides the drawbacks already mentioned, is copy error where data are drawn from the bicycle registration tax, as the figures were passed from one level of the bureaucracy to the next. If there were no data available because the registration tax was not due, the most plausible explanation is that figures are the result of an estimation process. It would be necessary to know exactly how the figures were compiled to understand the process of estimation and say something about the results. The sources usually do not provide any information about how they derived the figures, and it is thus very difficult to make any judgement. For example, data from 1898 to 1902 highlight a significant discrepancy among the available sources (Bertarelli 1900; Anonymous 1904; Roseo 1912) that presumably is explained through the tax evasion issue. This means that the source (Roseo 1912) had made some estimations to take into account the number of cyclists who did not pay the registration tax. In other cases, the sources clearly stated that they simply provided an estimate of bicycle ownership. This was the case for 1927 through 1932 (Vandone 1927b, 1934) and 1939 through 1955 (ANCMA 1953; Anonymous 1942; Roghi 1956). A further example is 1924, for which three different figures are available. Their size is very similar, except for one source (Anonymous 1924) that reported that the number of bicycles (2,264,105) referred to the first five months of 1924. The last example is 1959, which represents a completely different source (Luzzatto Fegiz 1960), as it is a survey conducted by a private firm engaged in public opinion research. The survey is based on a probability sample of the Italian population, and it provides a broader picture of bicycle ownership and the characteristics of Italian families that relate to bicycle ownership.

Bicycle ownership data in Japan do not allow a thorough analysis as that of Italy, nevertheless, it is useful to provide a brief discussion of the statistics available. The time series is from 1903 to 1977 and is drawn from two sources examined earlier in this chapter. The first source (Takeuchi 1991, pp. 122, 134) includes data from 1903 to 1909 and from 1916 to 1930. The second source (Ueda 1981, p. 61) provides data from 1913 through 1977. There are many inconsistencies between the sources and it is not possible to understand the reasons behind such a problem. The chart in Fig. 2.17 is created using both sources, but data from Ueda are preferred consistent with other statistics analysed earlier in this chapter.

The time series has a gap between 1910 and 1912. The graph shows that Japanese population adopted the bicycle at an increasing rate from the 1910s through the end of World War II reaching 8,556,000 units in 1944. Afterwards, the diffusion of bicycles was relentless until 1977 when approximately 46,800,000 units were widespread in the country.

2.6 Conclusion

The bicycle industry is about 150 years old and has tackled many complex problems, particularly those impacting the technology of the bicycle. Despite some great outcomes over time, the industry has not developed yet a suitable system for recording its statistics. The problems with current data are almost the same problems as those of the nascent industry. How to proceed for improving the situation? The chapter highlighted that various organizations play a role in providing bicycle statistics and it seems

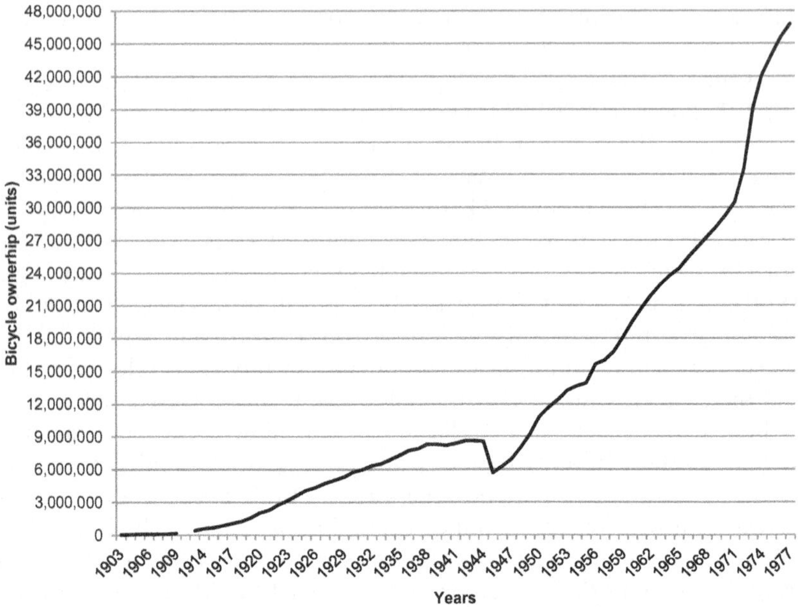

Fig. 2.17 Japanese bicycle ownership 1903–1977

clear that no one can afford to give up the contribution of the others in this endeavour. At the same time, it is also evident that there is a lack of coordination within those involved in gathering and compiling bicycle statistics. The coordination requires that the topic of bicycle statistics is included in the agenda of one or more of those organizations, as a priority to allow a more informed decision making within the whole industry. And the agenda setting, in turn, is based on the commitment to changing the way statistics are currently gathered. If no organizations express a strong commitment, the business as usual approach will perpetuate and bicycle statistics will still be affected by problems.

Gathering data can be a difficult and costly activity, however technology advancements such as the bar code and application programmes for mobile devices are a pragmatic course of action to address the problem of bicycle statistics. For instance, the trade organizations might promote the development of an International Standard Bicycle Number (ISBIN) similar to what is used in the publishing industry where each book has its own International Standard Book Number (ISBN). It is not an easy transition from the current system of bicycle statistics to a fully new approach. The technology is already available, what is missing is the commitment to change. Will any bicycle firm be willing to change its behaviour and declare how many bicycles were manufactured each year?

Another useful change regards foreign trade statistics. The chapter emphasized that one of the key problems remains the classification of goods adopted by customs agencies and developed by international organizations such as the European Union. These classifications keep changing and this is understandable since goods evolve over time, however a new edition should guarantee the comparability between same goods included in various versions of the classification. Moreover, code numbers to identify bicycle categories should be based on more digits, and should be harmonized all over the world, preventing the practice of each country to introduce their own code numbers. This change requires the action of international organizations, but it can be encouraged by trade organizations and their members, which might develop an agreed proposal to address the problem.

A further suggestion is for improving the availability and reliability of bicycle ownership statistics. It is advisable to perform a periodical survey to monitor how the relationship between citizens and bicycles develops over time in each country. This can be done through the office for national statistics or a private initiative promoted by trade organizations.

References

Accell Group N.V. (2005). *Accell annual report 2004*. Heerenveen, The Netherlands: Accell Group N.V.

Accell Group N.V. (2006). *Accell annual report 2005*. Heerenveen, The Netherlands: Accell Group N.V.

Accell Group N.V. (2007). *Accell annual report 2006*. Heerenveen, The Netherlands: Accell Group N.V.

Accell Group N.V. (2008). *Accell annual report 2007*. Heerenveen, The Netherlands: Accell Group N.V.

Accell Group N.V. (2009). *Accell annual report 2008*. Heerenveen, The Netherlands: Accell Group N.V.

Accell Group N.V. (2010). *Accell annual report 2009*. Heerenveen, The Netherlands: Accell Group N.V.

Accell Group N.V. (2011). *Accell annual report 2010*. Heerenveen, The Netherlands: Accell Group N.V.

Accell Group N.V. (2012). *Accell annual report 2011*. Heerenveen, The Netherlands: Accell Group N.V.
Accell Group N.V. (2013). *Accell annual report 2012*. Heerenveen, The Netherlands: Accell Group N.V.
Accell Group N.V. (2014). *Accell annual report 2013*. Heerenveen, The Netherlands: Accell Group N.V.
Accell Group N.V. (2015). *Accell annual report 2014*. Heerenveen, The Netherlands: Accell Group N.V.
Accell Group N.V. (2016). *Accell annual report 2015*. Heerenveen, The Netherlands: Accell Group N.V.
Accell Group N.V. (2017). *Accell annual report 2016*. Heerenveen, The Netherlands: Accell Group N.V.
Accell Group N.V. (2018). *Accell annual report 2017*. Heerenveen, The Netherlands: Accell Group N.V.
Accell Group N.V. (2019). *Accell annual report 2018*. Heerenveen, The Netherlands: Accell Group N.V.
Accell Group N.V. (2020). *Accell annual report 2019*. Heerenveen, The Netherlands: Accell Group N.V.
ANCMA. (1953). L'industria del ciclo e del motociclo. In Confederazione Generale dell'Industria Italiana (Ed.), *L'industria Italiana alla Metà del Secolo XX* (pp. 362–368). Rome, Italy: Tipografia del Senato.
ANCMA. (2019). *Produzione italiana serie storica*. Milan, Italy: Ancma.
ANCMA. (2020). *Dati mercato bici 2019*. Milan, Italy: Ancma.
Anonymous. (1903). Quanti sono i ciclisti in Italia. *Rivista Mensile del Touring Club Italiano, IX*(3), 98.
Anonymous. (1904). Statistica delle biciclette in Italia. *Rivista Mensile del Touring Club Italiano, X*(4), 130–131.
Anonymous. (1905). Quante sono le biciclette in Italia. *Rivista Mensile del Touring Club Italiano, XI*(1), 12.
Anonymous. (1924). L'aumento delle biciclette, motociclette e automobili in Italia. *Le Vie d'Italia, XXX*(11), 1255.
Anonymous. (1926). Statistica delle automobili, motociclette e biciclette circolanti in Italia nel 1925. *Le Vie d'Italia, XXXII*(11), 1265.
Anonymous. (1936). Statistica delle biciclette circolanti in Italia nel 1933, 1934 e 1935. *Le Vie d'Italia, XLII*(8), 324.
Anonymous. (1937). Statistica delle biciclette circolanti in Italia nel 1935 e 1936. *Le Vie d'Italia, XLIII*(9), 425.
Anonymous. (1938). Statistica delle biciclette circolanti in Italia nel 1937. *Le Vie d'Italia, XLIV*(8), 1034–1035.
Anonymous. (1939). La circolazione ciclistica del 1938 in rapporto alla popolazione delle provincie. *Le Vie d'Italia, XLV*(9), 1283–1284.

Anonymous. (1942). L'unificazione delle parti di bicicletta. *Le Vie D'Italia, XLVIII*(3), 240–241.

Babaian, S. (1998). *The most benevolent machine: A historical assessment of cycles in Canada*. Ottawa, ON, Canada: National Museum of Science and Technology.

Bertarelli, L. V. (1900). Statistica istruttiva. *Rivista Mensile Del Touring Club Ciclistico Italiano, VI*(1), 8–9.

Bertarelli, L. V. (1915). Vent'anni di un sodalizio nazionale. Il Touring Club Italiano. *Nuova Antologia di Lettere, Scienze ed Arti, V*(1–2), 24–52.

Bianchi, A. G. (1901). Verso la targhetta mobile. *Rivista Mensile Del Touring Club Italiano, VII*(11), 334–335.

Bianchi, A. G. (1908). Per la bicicletta. *Rivista Mensile del Touring Club Italiano, XIV*(11), 499–504.

Biffi, C. (1941). I veicoli in Italia. *Le Strade, XXIII*(7), 336–338.

Brentari, O. (1902). Quanti sono i ciclisti in Italia. *Rivista Mensile Del Touring Club Italiano, VIII*(3), 77–79.

Ceriani, A. (1926). Automobili, motocicli e biciclette nel 1924. *Le Vie D'Italia, XXXII*(1), 1–11.

Chu, W., & Li, J. (1996). Growth and industrial organization. A comparative study of the bicycle industry in Taiwan and South Korea. *Journal of Industry Studies, 3*(1), 35–52.

Chu, W., & Li, J. (1997). Causes of growth: A study of Taiwan's bicycle industry. *Cambridge Journal of Economics, 21*(1), 55–72.

Customs Administration of Taiwan. (2020). *Trade statistics*. Taipei City, Taiwan: Statistics Office.

Epperson, B. (2001). How many bikes? An investigation into the quantification of bicycling 1878–1914. In I. A. Boal & A. Ritchie (Eds.), *Cycle History 11. Proceedings of the 11th International Cycling History Conference* (pp. 42–50). Verona, NJ: The ICHC Publications Committee.

Epperson, B. (2012). *Revised bicycle production figures* (Unpublished manuscript, pp. 1–2).

Gazzaniga, L. (1935). Il giubileo della bicicletta. *Le Vie D'Italia, XLI*(7), 541–547.

Istituto Nazionale di Statistica. (2020). *Coeweb. Statistiche del commercio estero*. Rome, Italy: ISTAT.

Japan Association of Bicycle Manufacturers. (1979). *Overview of the bicycle industry*. Tokyo, Japan: Nihon Jitensha Kyokai.

Japan Bicycle Promotion Institute. (2019). *Japanese bicycle production, import and export. Twelve-month year to date 2018*. Tokyo, Japan: JBPI.

Johnson, F. (1896). A sua eccellenza il Ministro delle Finanze. *Rivista Mensile Del Touring Club Ciclistico Italiano, II*(2), 18–22.

Kotha, S., & Fried, A. (1993). *The national bicycle industrial company: Implementing a strategy of mass customization*. New York, NY: New York University and International University of Japan Case Series.

Luzzatto Fegiz, P. (1960). Le biciclette in Italia. *Bollettino della Doxa, XIV*(17), 165–178.

Mari, C. (2018). Bicycle statistics in Italy. In G. W. Sanderson (Ed.), *Cycle History 29. Proceedings of the 29th International Cycling History Conference* (pp. 190–195). Verona, NJ: The ICHC Publications Committee.

Millward, A. (1999). *Factors contributing to the sustained success of the UK cycle industry 1870–1939*. PhD thesis, University of Birmingham.

Ministry of Economic Affairs of Taiwan. (2020). *Industrial statistics*. Taipei City, Taiwan: Department of Statistics.

Nigrelli, P. (2018, February 7). Personal communication.

Piloni, R. (1982). *Un settore industriale in sviluppo: L'industria della bicicletta dalla fine dell'Ottocento al 1914*. Master thesis, University of Milan.

Roghi, B. (1956). Tramonto della bicicletta? *Le Vie D'Italia, LXII*(7), 891–897.

Rosen, P. (2002). *Framing production. Technology, culture, and change in the British bicycle industry*. Cambridge, MA: The MIT Press.

Roseo, G. G. (1912). *L'industria e il commercio dei velocipedi nel mondo*. Milan, Italy: Libreria Editrice Milanese.

Spaventa Filippi, G. (1927). Automobili, motocicli, biciclette nel 1925. *Le Vie D'Italia, XXXIII*(1), 52–56.

Takeuchi, T. (1991). The bicycle industry. In T. Takeuchi (Ed.), *The role of labour-intensive sectors in Japanese industrialization* (pp. 112–163). Tokyo, Japan: The United Nations University.

The Department of Finance. (n.d.a). *1917 Annual return of the foreign trade of the Empire of Japan*. Tokyo, Japan: The Department of Finance.

The Department of Finance. (n.d.b). *1930 Annual return of the foreign trade of the Empire of Japan*. Tokyo, Japan: The Department of Finance.

Ueda, T. (1981). *The development of the bicycle industry in Japan after World War II*. Tokyo, Japan: The United Nations University.

Vandone, I. (1927a). Statistica degli autoveicoli per l'anno 1925. *Le Strade, IX*(2), 37–40.

Vandone, I. (1927b). L'automobilismo in Italia 1925–1926. *Le Strade, IX*(7), 149–154.

Vandone, I. (1930). Laude della bicicletta. *Le Vie D'Italia, XXXVI*(4), 254–258.

Vandone, I. (1934). Che ne facciamo del ciclista? *Le Strade, XVI*(6), 322–324.

Vandone, I. (1935). Lo sviluppo del ciclismo in Italia. *Le Strade, XVII*(9), 527–529.

CHAPTER 3

Marketing the Bicycle

Abstract How does the practice of marketing work within the bicycle industry? This chapter examines the bicycle marketing focusing on its three pillars, which consist of understanding customers through market segmentation, designing a market offering for those customers who bicycle firms choose to serve and using sports as a marketing tool. For each topic, the chapter discusses the evolution of marketing practice since the birth of the bicycle industry. Furthermore, the chapter is enriched through examples, based on data, showing market segmentation approaches, market offering hierarchies and participation by bicycle firms to key stage-races on the road.

Keywords Market segment · Segmentation variable · Product line · Model · Product variant · Annual model change · Road racing

3.1 Marketing in the Bicycle Industry

The bicycle industry and marketing have a curious relationship from a historical perspective. They are both victims of a twofold neglect. Firstly, the role played by marketing in understanding the evolution of an industry is underrated. Economic and business historians usually approach the study of an industry from a technological perspective. The main focus is technological innovation and its impact on industries over time.

C. Mari, *A Business History of the Bicycle Industry*,
https://doi.org/10.1007/978-3-030-50563-9_3

This is the supply side perspective emphasizing the changes in production brought by technology. It is evident that technological innovations have been the keys to the industrial revolutions since the eighteenth century, nevertheless, this idea neglects an alternative perspective that calls for including the demand side into the history of any industry. It means that consumers do play a role in shaping the success or failure of a new product developed through technological innovation. Since the eighteenth century, consumers had to be persuaded that they needed the new products launched into the market. This situation indicated that manufacturing was not enough to pursue a firm's goals. A further activity was needed to handle the demand side of the business. It was marketing and it worked in tandem with manufacturing to enhance the demand for new offerings (Fullerton 1988, p. 112). Bicycle industry studies are no exception since most of them favour the technological perspective as the main lens for understanding the evolution over time. Marketing is very often a neglected topic within bicycle history literature. Secondly, the role played by the bicycle industry in developing marketing innovations, which impacted on other industries, particularly the automobile industry, has been almost completely ignored (Petty 1995, p. 33). Bicycle industry was instrumental in bringing about modern marketing as it is known nowadays. Marketing historians tend to focus on other consumer goods such as food, beverages, detergents, toiletries and cosmetics, home appliances and cars. It seems difficult to acknowledge the contribution of bicycle industry in advancing marketing concepts and tools, which are still used in many industries all over the world.

Bicycle marketing was involved in building the underpinnings of the automobile age by providing a preview on a miniature scale of much of the social phenomena which the automobile enlarged upon (Aronson 1952, p. 312). The bicycle and the marketing activities created to enhance its demand had, directly and indirectly, a decided influence on the introduction and ready acceptance of the automobile (Oliver and Berkebile 1974, pp. 22–24). The attractiveness of the automobile was nourished on the feeling inspired by the bicycle, which extended the boundaries of spatial experience for the consumers and stimulated desires for increased independence of movement. This experience was the background for considering motor vehicles, particularly small cars, as the obvious next stage in searching for increased mobility (Sachs 1992, p. 106). It was the bicycle that gave rise to a new type of mobility, introducing thousands of people to individual and independent mechanical transportation, which became widespread during the twentieth century through the automobile. The bicycle and its marketing rendered another service to future car drivers by forming a movement for road repairs and construction in the United States. This was a lobbying group, called Good Roads movement, which succeeded in promoting the construction of hundreds of miles of roads upon which the early automobile depended, and the creation of both state and federal legislation that would result in the national highway system (Hounshell 1979, p. 180).

The marketing of bicycles also provided the automobile industry with a distribution system based on a network of both agents and repair shops where selling and repairing were carried out. These shops also acted as a training school for a group of mechanics who could easily turn from the bicycle to the automobile (Aronson 1952, p. 310). In UK some of the leading bicycle firms, such as Humber, Rover, Singer, Swift, Triumph and BSA began to make motor cars and took advantage of their distribution system, which already existed (Church 1982, p. 7). A similar situation happened in the United States for some bicycle builders, such as Albert A. Pope, Alexander Winton and George N. Pierce (Chandler 1964, pp. 10–11). The large number of bicycle dealers in the 1900s, in Europe and the United States, helped the nascent automobile industry to search for its cadre of dealers within the bicycle industry. For instance, the first dealer of Ford Motor Company was an agent for a bicycle firm (Tedlow 1990, p. 134). The link between bicycle dealers and car dealers was so strong that a study about the marketing of automobiles, conducted in the 1910s in US, divided the car dealers into three categories: bicycle men, nephew of rich uncles, and men seeking new connections (Tedlow 1990, p. 136). Overall, the marketing of bicycles was a learning experience for the car culture of the twentieth century (Hounshell 1979, p. 179) and contributed to the development of the system of *automobility* described by Sheller and Urry (2000).

This chapter intends to remedy the shortcomings of a twofold neglect, mentioned earlier, through the analysis of what marketing was, and still is, within the bicycle industry. Marketing is about the interplay between company and customer within the context of competition (Tedlow 1990, p. 375), and, to manage this interaction, a bicycle firm can employ various marketing concepts and tools. The chapter focuses on the three interdependent pillars that are the core marketing activities practised by bicycle firms. Firstly, segmenting the market; secondly, developing a variety of offerings; and thirdly, using sports as a marketing tool. Bicycle marketing is more than these three pillars, but its very nature is deep-rooted in them, and it is fair to say that there is no marketing without them. The other marketing concepts and tools used within the bicycle industry depend on them and need to be consistent with them. The following sections examine each of the three pillars.

3.2 Segmenting Markets

It is plausible that the bicycle industry used a form of market segmentation since its birth in the 1870s, but the introduction of the safety bicycle was the watershed for adopting a more advanced way of segmenting markets. The new approach was a marketing strategy characterized by a customer-centred mind-set. Does it mean that bicycle firms understood that customers played an essential role in determining the success or failure of the new bicycle, and, as a result, asked themselves which potential customers should we attempt to serve? The answer was the process of market segmentation, which consists of dividing the market into groups of potential customers, called market segments, with distinct characteristics, behaviours, needs, or wants. Segmentation aims to cluster customers in groups that clearly differ from each other but show a great deal of homogeneity within the group. It is important that the segments are sufficiently different from each other. Companies chose which market segments to serve and develop a specific offering for each. Segment-based marketing is usually compared with its alternative—mass marketing—that does not recognize the diversity of customers, and consequently develops the same offering for all customers.

Market segmentation is an essential component of the history of marketing, particularly marketing practice (Fullerton 2016). This history is usually framed according to the three phases in the development of consumer product marketing in the Unites States (Tedlow 1990). Tedlow argues that it is possible to discern a progression in American marketing through three phases: fragmentation, unification and segmentation. His structured periodization is built on the evidence drawn from four industries: soft drinks, automobiles, grocery retailing and general merchandise retailing. The market segmentation phase began approximately in the 1920s for the automobile industry and later, during the 1950s, for most consumer goods industries. This historical account was criticized by other scholars that considered his three-phase model too simplistic (Cohen 1990, p. 552; Trentmann 2017, p. 317). One of the main criticisms was that market segmentation was already practised before the period of time indicated by Tedlow. He replied arguing that the segmentation that took place after World War II was far more complex than anything that had preceded it. Before the 1950s, there had been a market segmentation based on price through which firms would offer three lines (known as good, better, and best) of an essentially similar product. Since the 1950s, market segmentation, instead of relying on price or product characteristics, was based on telling the customer what kind of person buys the kind of offering in question. This form of market segmentation was designed to create a community of customers (Tedlow 2015, pp. 25–26). Tedlow clearly states that his phases of marketing evolution are applied to non-American markets, and to a range of products, and sometimes found useful, and sometimes not (Tedlow and Jones 2015, p. 7). However, he does not acknowledge the role played by the bicycle industry in developing a complex form of market segmentation between the 1890s and the 1900s, which impacted on the automobile industry and, plausibly, other industries.

How was the bicycle market segmented? The answer is provided by the catalogues and price lists, from 1899 to 1954, of the most long-lived Italian bicycle firm: the Bianchi company (Mari 2015, pp. 142–144). This firm was a market leader and it is plausible to state that its segmentation approach represented a common practice within the bicycle industry in Italy and abroad, as corroborated by other sources such as the catalogues and price lists of the Rover Cycle Company Limited (1897) or The Raleigh Cycle Co. Ltd. (1889, 1906).

During the early 1900s, the bicycle industry used two broad criteria to divide customers into segments: demographic and behavioural characteristics. The former criterion relied upon the following specific variables: gender, age and anthropometric measures. The latter used two further variables: bicycle usage and price sensitivity. The application of these criteria to segment the market can be thought as a sequence of steps (Fig. 3.1). The first is to use the variable *gender* to identify two segments: male customers and female customers. The second step was to apply the variable *age* to the previous segments and group four new segments: adult male customers, children male customers, adult female customers and children female customers. The third step was to add the *bicycle usage*, a behavioural characteristic, to identify new segments of customers. The main uses for bicycle were transportation, leisure and racing. Each of them is linked to a specific group of customers: commuters, tourists, and racers

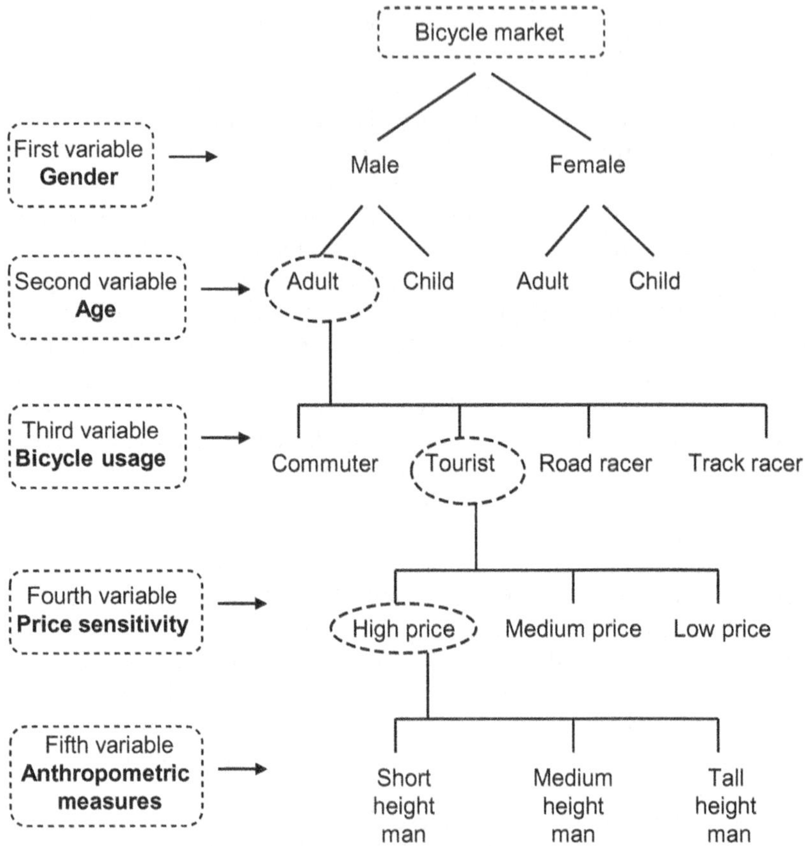

Fig. 3.1 Bicycle market segmentation in the 1900s

who were further subdivided into road and track racers. To exemplify a partial list of new segments were adult male commuters, adult male tourists, adult male road racers and adult male track racers. The fourth step in market segmentation was to examine *price sensitivity* of customers. It meant to acknowledge that customers showed further key differences in regard to income and social class. The bicycle industry used a price range to take into account socioeconomic conditions of customers and develop offerings consistent with what each market segment could afford to buy. A partial example of new segments based on three levels of price was:

adult male tourists able to pay a high price, adult male tourists able to pay a medium price, and adult male tourists able to pay a low price. The last step in segmenting the market was to use the ***anthropometric measures***. These are the human body measurements affecting the size of the bicycle that, in turn, influences the performance of the cyclist in pedalling. The new segments resulting from the use of anthropometric measures were classified according to the height, or stature, of the potential customers usually measured in centimetres. The height was considered as a synthesis of the basic anthropometric dimensions such as thigh length, lower leg length, inseam length, chest height, upper arm length, forearm length and hand length. The height was easier to measure and gave a rough idea of bicycle fit to a specific customer. For example, the segment including adult male tourists able to pay a high price was subdivided into three new segments, each of them corresponding to a different height: short height man, medium height man and tall height man. It should be emphasized that bicycle industry preferred to convert the height of customers into the size of the bicycle frame, usually measured in centimetres, so that market segments were identified through small, medium and large bicycle frame. Instead, for children bicycles the size of the wheels was used as a proxy for anthropometric measures. It was usually measured in inches, for example, 20 and 24 inch wheel diameter. Figure 3.1 exemplifies the adult male segment using the bicycle for tourism and able to pay a high price for a bicycle. The other market segments follow the same logic.

The previous complex segmentation scheme identified multiple segments that needed to be evaluated from the perspective of the company to decide which of them to serve and which to ignore. The rationale was that some market segments were less attractive for fulfilling firm goals and, consequently, it was not feasible to develop a unique offering for each segment. The company retained those market segments for which it was able to create an offering that satisfied customer needs better than the competition and, at the same time, achieved its goals. The final result was the product assortment as it appeared in the company catalogues that hid the segmentation criteria and emphasized the offering.

After almost 120 years, how has the segmentation of the bicycle market changed? The answer is straightforward: nothing has changed. To find evidence of such a statement is enough to take a close look at any catalogue and price list (print or online) published by a bicycle firm. This is an easy way to discover the market segmentation employed by the bicycle industry. In most cases, catalogues and price lists provide all the information required to grasp the market segmentation variables hidden by the product assortment. The example below is drawn from the 2011 catalogue and price list of Giant Manufacturing Co. Ltd., the leading Taiwanese firm, which allow a thorough comparison with the market segmentation approach of the 1900s. The Giant's segmentation framework shares both the five variables and the sequence of steps with the market segmentation process discussed earlier. Firstly, the bicycle market is divided into three groups according to two demographic variables: gender and age (Giant 2010a). This step leads to three market segments: adult men, adult women and youth (both female and male). Secondly, Giant employs two behavioural variables for each market segment: bicycle usage and price sensitivity. To understand both variables, Giant asks its potential customers the following questions: (a) where do you ride?, which provides a clue to bicycle usage; (b) what is your desired riding level?, which helps to shed light about how customers are sensitive to price. The former question has three alternatives answers: on road (that is, paved roads and paths), off road (that is, single track and dirt paths), and across-the-road (that is, a mix of dirt and pavement). The latter question has also three alternative answers: lifestyle, sport and performance. These three riding levels correspond to different price points within the offering (Giant 2010b). It means that a lifestyle customer is interested in a less expensive bicycle, a performance customer is willing to spend a lot of money for buying a bicycle, and a sport customer is in-between the other riding levels. The three alternative answers to each question can be arranged in a two-dimensional matrix of nine cells, each representing a market segment (Fig. 3.2). For example, the group of customers including adult men riding off road and enthusiasts of expensive mountain bicycles (that is, a performance riding level). Figure 3.2 depicts the matrix for the adult men segment, which is slightly different for women and youth segments. The matrix for women has eight cells since Giant is not serving the market segment identified as across-the-road and performance. The youth matrix includes only three cells: on road and lifestyle, off road and sport, and across-the-road and performance. The third and last step in the market segmentation process is to consider the anthropometric measures. Giant manufactures various sizes of both bicycle frame and wheel for each of the cells within the three matrixes.

Apparently, the two market segmentation approaches might be considered different from each other. There is a partial variation in wordings and

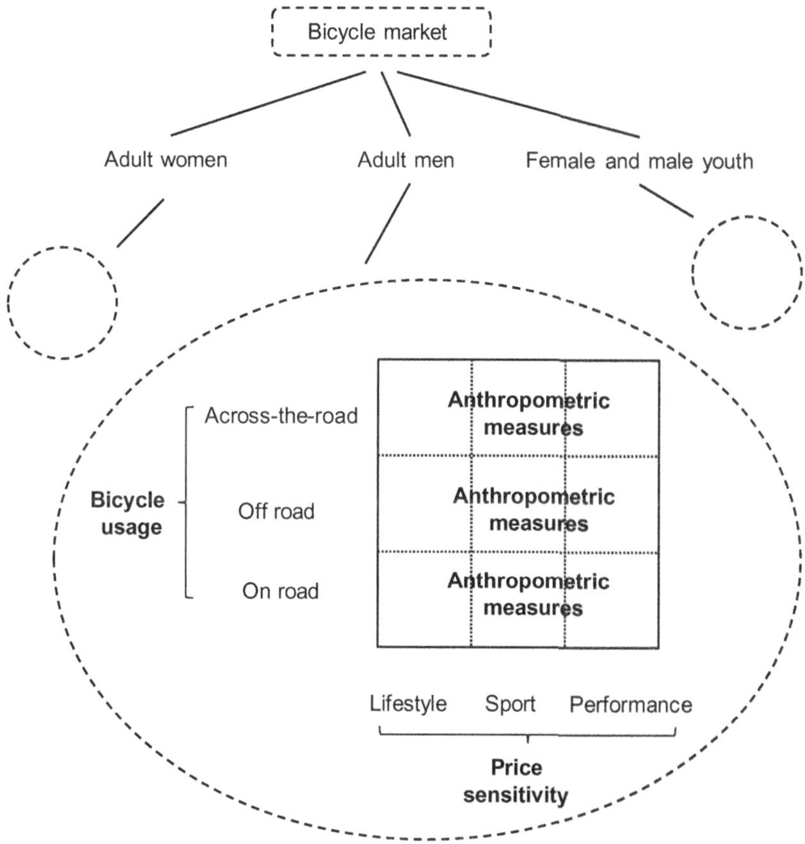

Fig. 3.2 Bicycle market segmentation in the 2010s

the process of jointly applying the variables to identify market segments, employed by Giant, could be seen as a different option by a careless reader of company catalogues. These differences are minor points that do not change the basic framework shared by both approaches. It is fair to state that market segmentation in the bicycle industry is still done in the same way as it was since the 1900s. Both examples of segmentation clearly show that the argument regarding the three phases of marketing evolution, and particularly the segmentation phase, does not hold. Market segmentation was a practice already used before the 1920s and it was also a complex approach based on both demographic and behavioural variables. Bicycle firms learned very early that product characteristics or price were not enough for identifying potential customers, something else was needed. Bicycle usage, as a further market segmentation variable, helped bicycle firms to focus on the desire of potential cyclists for being part of a community of customers sharing the same interest in cycling. For those cyclists, buying a specific kind of bicycle was a way to be associated with a distinct group of customers, such as the commuters using their bicycle on road, the tourists riding across-the-road, or the racers competing off road. This emphasis on the identification of a person with a broader group of customers has received a renewed attention, within the bicycle industry, through the variable gender. In 2008, Giant opened its first store exclusively for women, called *Liv / giant*, in Taipei City on the assumption that this distinct group of potential cyclists was neglected compared to men. Three years later, in 2011, Giant launched *Liv / giant* as a new brand of bicycles dedicated to serving female riders worldwide, and changed its name to *Liv* in 2020.

3.3 Developing Market Offerings

The second pillar of bicycle marketing centres around what products a firm should offer for sale and what features they should incorporate. These choices are usually called product policy decisions. They are intertwined with market segmentation as they follow it. Once a bicycle firm identifies market segments, it has to decide which of them it wants to serve and how. Product policy in the bicycle industry has been characterized by two main decisions: creating variety in market offerings and managing it over time.

The former decision involves what and how many products to offer. It means that bicycle firms choose the dimensions of variety to compete on, which must be of value to customers. Variety refers to the number of items within the offering of a firm. Offerings are also called product assortment, product mix, product range or collection. Variety is a stock concept that is bound to a specific set of items and a moment in time (Sanderson and Uzumeri 1997, p. 9). It is measured at a given time through the mapping of existing products, which is a hierarchical structure showing the relationship between the items of the offering. This hierarchy is organized into three levels: product lines, models (also called products) and product variants (also called items, versions or stock-keeping unit, SKU). A single product line usually includes a group of models that are closely related because they are proposed to the same market segment and perform a similar function. A single model differs sufficiently from other models and has a distinctive marketing designation within the marketplace. It usually consists of a group of product variants. A single item is distinguishable by size, appearance, or components. The offering of a bicycle firm can be measured through three dimensions: the number of product lines, the number of models within each product line, and the number of product variants of each model. Bicycle firms usually divide up their product lines very finely, with each model representing a small variation from the rest of the line. Thus, bicycle firms extend their offerings with only incremental changes and manufacture multiple models with highly similar components (Dowell 2006, p. 962).

To examine further the concept of variety within an offering, it can be useful to categorize it into three types: fit, taste and quality (Ulrich 2005, p. 115). Each of them refers to one or more characteristics of the bicycle. For instance, a fit characteristic is the size of the bicycle frame or the size of wheels. A fit characteristic is based on the interaction between the customer and the product, which, in turn, affects the degree of customer satisfaction or dissatisfaction in using the bicycle. Metaphorically, a cyclist should wear the bicycle as a piece of clothing. Fit characteristics recall the anthropometric measures employed to segment markets, and explain why bicycle firms use this category of variety in their offerings. A taste characteristic is the colour of the bicycle or the brand of some components. Customers show their preferences for a particular taste characteristic that can influence the decision to buy or not to buy the bicycle. Variety based on taste characteristics is a further key decision in developing market offerings that are appealing to customers. A quality characteristic refers to variation in quality levels of bicycles. It is usually created within a product line to take into account the price sensitivity of customers. It is used to establish a price-performance link between the bicycles in the same product line. It means that the variety stems from the price range of components used for manufacturing the models within the product line. Thus, less expensive components offer a lower level of performance, and more expensive components provide a higher performance level. It is a common practice to build a product line through several models starting from an economy model (or low-end, or low-quality), and ending to a premium model (or high-end, or high-quality).

The linkage between segmentation criteria and offering is that product lines are built for market segments identified through gender, age, and bicycle usage. Whereas models are developed for accounting for price sensitivity of segments and product variants try to fit the anthropometric measures of customers or satisfy other needs and wants. The following examples provide some evidence about the offerings of the two bicycle firms discussed earlier.

In 1902 Bianchi's offering consisted of six product lines, twelve models, and sixty seven product variants (Mari 2015, pp. 145–146). Four product lines were for segments interested in using the bicycle for transportation and leisure purposes and two for racing activity. It is likely to assume that despite the fact that commuting and leisure riding were different market segments, Bianchi company decided it was not viable to offer specific models for each of them and developed an offering suitable for both purposes. The four product lines for transportation and leisure were: bicycles for adult males, bicycles for adult females, bicycles for boys and bicycles for girls. The two further product lines were: bicycles for adult males engaged in road racing and bicycles for adult males practising track racing. Each product line consisted of a certain number of models and it is evident that adult male segments were the most important for Bianchi. Three out of six product lines and seven out of twelve models were developed for them. Moreover, commuting and leisure riding of adult men was considered the main field of usage requiring the most models. Specifically, such a product line included seven models whose price range was from 350 to 680 lire. Each model was identified through a letter or a technical characteristic and for each of them were available some product variants according to what the company thought was appropriate. For instance, model *B* was offered in four different frame sizes and customers could also choose two different braking systems. The total number of product variants within the man commuting and leisure product line was 39.

The structure of offering proposed in 1902 resembled the basic product assortment developed by the company from 1899 to 1954. Each year between five and seven product lines were available. The transportation and leisure bicycles for man, woman, boy, and girl, were the four main product lines offered to a broad public, whereas the other key product line represented by road racing bicycles was for a niche group of enthusiasts. Two further product lines were not available every year because they fulfilled a very particular customer need. The track racing bicycles were offered from 1899 to the 1920s. This was consistent with the evolution of cycling that gradually replaced track races with road racing events. The seventh product line was developed for military purposes in the early 1910s. From 1899 to 1954, the Bianchi product lines offered between seven and seventeen models each year. Most of the time there were eleven models, with between 60 and 80% of the offering aimed at the key market segment of adult males. Moreover, the bicycles used by adult men for transportation and leisure riding represented between 40 and 60% of the product assortment. Models within the same product line were delineated on a price-performance basis. The higher the price, the greater the performance of the bicycle. Bicycles varied in their performance on different attributes. It was usually technical features that impacted the weight of the bicycle, its comfort, or its style. Bianchi tried to appeal to consumers from various income and social classes through luxury and affordable products. The former were expensive bicycles comprising advanced features such as a lighter steel for building the frame or a more effective braking system. The latter were inexpensive bicycles that offered a basic set of features consistent with a low price. In 1902 Bianchi proposed 67 product variants, 62 in 1914, 38 in 1933 and 42 in 1941. Most of the time Bianchi offered three different frame sizes, measured in centimetres, for its main products. In the late 1920s, the number of frame sizes of male bicycles used for transportation and leisure was up to six.

The Giant's offering in 2011 consisted of 20 product lines, 133 models, and 560 product variants (Giant 2010a, b). There was a product line for each market segment served by the company as depicted in Fig. 3.3, which includes the market segmentation approach examined earlier. Each matrix refers to a broad group of potential customers: adult men, adult women, and female and male youth. Giant decided to serve the nine market segments of adult men identified through bicycle usage and price sensitivity. At the same time, some market segments of adult women and youth were not considered promising for the company, and no offering was developed for them. Each cell of the matrixes includes the number of models.

The whole offering of Giant in 2011 shared the same emphasis on adult men customers as of Bianchi's offering. Over 70% of models available were for adult men, compared to approximately 16% for adult women and 14% for youth. A similar situation is confirmed by the number of product variants: 80% for adult men, 16% for adult women and 4% for

	Adult men			Adult women			Youth female and male		
	L	S	P	L	S	P	L	S	P
Across-the-road	1	4	2	1	2				3
Off road	5	5	35	2	1	2		6	
On road	12	8	22	6	3	4	9		

L = Lifestyle S = Sport P = Performance

Fig. 3.3 Offering of Giant in 2011

youth. The matrix of adult men shows that most of the models are developed for being used on road and off road. Moreover, customers able to spend more money for buying a bicycle can choose from a larger variety of models as the performance riding level, both on road and off road, has the highest number of models and product variants. The variety of offering is created through fit and quality characteristics. Giant developed from one to six sizes of a bicycle frame, depending on the price range of the bicycle. The more expensive the model, the more sizes of a bicycle frame. The quality characteristic was extensively used to provide customers with a selection of price points that could satisfy a large number of potential customers. The taste characteristic, based on the colour of bicycles, was not very common in Giant's offering. Most of the bicycles were offered in one colour and very few of them had two or three options, usually the less expensive bicycles.

The second decision of product policy, in the bicycle industry, is managing variety over time. This choice is usually framed as the annual model change approach. The origin of this practice is controversial (Petty 1995, p. 40), some scholars argue that it was used by the nascent bicycle industry in UK while others maintain that it originated from other durable goods industries. There are traces of this practice in four industries and examining them might provide a clue to the puzzle of its origin.

The farm implement industry in the United States, from the late 1840s to the 1850s, began to change every part of their machines from years to years, particularly the McCormick reaper company used to change its whole offering of machines every year to keep them attractive in the market. The changes were dictated by the presence of competition, and by the experimental work in progress to improve the products. The annual model change within this industry became a pattern for both manufacturers and farmers, who came to expect changes from year to year. The industry was characterized by a habitual cycle of change (Hounshell 1984, pp. 157–159).

The pottery and glass industry in the United States introduced, by the 1880s, the practice of changing some products at the beginning of each year. The potters and glassmakers began to launch new patterns every year to capture the trade of high-volume customers. They understood that it was more effective to do business with department stores, chain stores and mail-order houses. As a result, a new approach to product design, innovation and promotion was developed. It was mainly based on introducing some new products every year, and creating artistic items in a hierarchy of price categories to accommodate customer preferences and differences. Moreover the industry participated to the annual show ran, in early January, in Pittsburgh. This event became the way to institutionalize the annual model change practice (Lee Blaszczyk 2000, pp. 24–26). US pottery and glass industry emulated the example of the British firm Wedgwood & Bentley, which developed, during the eighteenth century, a set of marketing practices for satisfying the demand of the people for novelty and beauty, such as introducing one or two new shapes or patterns every year and using a showroom in a fashionable quarter of London (McKendrick 1982).

The British bicycle industry started to renew its offerings every year during the 1880s (Harrison 1977, pp. 113–117; Millward 1999, pp. 167–169; Duncans 1898, p. 506). It meant that the whole offering was changed every year according to an established seasonal pattern, which included the participation to an annual show, such as the Stanley Show, which ran from 1878, and later the National Show, which ran from 1893. The quest for novelty arose from both the process of product invention and refinement, which was continuous until the basic design of the bicycle settled down around the safety bicycle, and the need to expand the market through the extension of the practice of cycling to new classes and purposes. The annual model change was also nourished by the buying habits of potential customers who showed a desire for constant change, which, in turn, was shaped by the pressure of fashion. For instance, in Italy during the 1910s most of the cyclists bought a new bicycle every three years compared to seven-eight years of the 1890s, and some affluent people could afford to buy a new bicycle every year or even twice a year (Roseo 1912, p. 202).

The automobile industry, particularly the General Motors Corporation, introduced the annual model change practice in the 1920s. It was Alfred P. Sloan, Jr, who became operating vice-president of General Motors in 1921 and president in 1923, who gave birth to this practice (Tedlow 1990, pp. 167–168). He developed a broader product policy based on three aspects: the product line, the annual model change and style. This was the answer to the competition facing the automobile industry by the mid-1920s in the United States. Marketing became a greater challenge than production and the main problem was no longer to sell an individual his first car, but to convince him who already owned a car to buy a new car (Chandler 1964, p. 13). It was also coined the word *Sloanism* to evoke such product policy, even though it was not so widespread as it was *Fordism* (Rothschild 1973, p. 38). The offering of General Motors was organized in a six-model price range that ran incrementally from cheap to expensive. Each model was launched at a selected price point within the specified price range. These price points had to be sufficiently separated to prevent the company from competing primarily against itself (Tedlow 1990, p. 169). Sloan reasoned that the price range structure would fully accommodate potential buyers of every income throughout their lives. This is an example of market segmentation implemented through the variable price, and it seems that General Motors did not use further variables to understand its markets (Tedlow 1990, p. 180). The annual model change initiated in 1923, but the concept evolved gradually and was fully formalized and regularized in the 1930s. Sloan recalled that 'on the average two years elapse between the time we make the first decisions on the new models and the time the cars appear in dealers' showrooms' (Sloan 1990 [1963], p. 238). The changes had to be done between the first of August and the first of November as any other date run into the selling season (Sloan 1990 [1963], p. 167), and were primarily based on style. The role of styling was to change car bodies on a four-year cycle, with face-lifting changes in-between (Sloan 1990 [1963], p. 277). The appearance of a car was considered the most important factor in convincing customers that the car they presently owned was obsolete. As a result, the annual model change was the ideal device to stimulate car sales and claim that last year's model was no longer in fashion.

The annual model change practice has different meanings in different industries. Its scope ranges from genuine improvements employed through structural changes, which affect the performance of a product, to cosmetic upgrades based on stylistic and aesthetic changes to make the product seem new or different. Its application can involve the whole offering each year or a part of it. For instance, both farm implement and bicycle industries renewed the full offering every year, whereas pottery and automobile industries focused their changes on a limited number of products. The bicycle industry usually uses the expression annual collection to indicate that changes are implemented across the whole product assortment. The possibility to change the offering from one year to another was made easier by using interchangeable components and sharing them across a wide range of bicycles. The four industries show that the main rationale behind the annual model change practice was to increase the sales of a product. However, they also emphasize the role played by potential customers who asked for novelty and changes. It is plausible to state that there was a dialogue between customers and firms. Product policy decided by those firms shaped consumer preferences, but at the same time, those preferences influenced the choices made by the firms. Both behaviours contributed to make the annual model change a habit within those industries.

3.4 Marketing Through Sports

The third pillar of marketing in the bicycle industry is the use of sports as a marketing tool. It should be emphasized that marketing through sports is different from sports marketing. The former means that bicycle manufacturers use sports activity as the basis for appeal to potential customers of their products. The sports activity is part of the firms' marketing efforts to market bicycles. The latter is the application of marketing concepts and tools to market sporting events and to increase the number of participants, both athletes and spectators, in a specific sporting activity. Bicycle firms are not sports organizations whose primary goals are organizing sporting events or promoting the practice of competitive cycling.

It might help to briefly recall what bicycle sports means. Bicycle racing emerged in the 1870s and 1880s and evolved from the classic form of sprinting on the track, held in hippodromes or on special tracks constructed for cycling, to a new kind of racing based on four categories of events: long-distance place-to-place races on the road, stage-races on the road, *stayer* or paced races on the track, and Six-Day races on the track (Ritchie 2018, p. 265). Long-distance road races were introduced in the late 1880s and early 1890s. Cyclists had to race over a distance of 500 or 600 km, with no scheduled rest-breaks, aiming to cover the distance in as short a time as possible. For example, some European road races still take place nowadays, such as Liège-Bastogne-Liège, first held in 1890, or Paris-Roubaix, since 1896. A stage-race is a race held over several days, consisting of separate daily races with aggregate finishing time (Ritchie 2018, pp. 267–269). The two most well-known examples of this kind of bicycle racing, which still take place on a regular basis, are the Tour de France, first held in 1903, and the Giro d'Italia, since 1909. A paced race evokes the athletic technique by which one cyclist benefits by riding in the slipstream either of another single cyclist, a multi-cycle or a motor-driven pacing machine, which made it possible for cyclists to overcome wind-resistance and ride faster (Ritchie 2018, p. 272). Six-Days were indoor track races lasting for six days, in which either individuals or teams of two riders competed (Ritchie 2018, p. 277). Road races became the most widespread form of bicycle racing and are still the emblem of modern competitive cycling.

Why bicycle racing and its four categories of events were of interest to the bicycle industry? The answer might appear obvious, but the relationship between the industry and the sports was complex and has affected the history of bicycle business until today. A clue to answer the question is provided by the vision of the founder of Bianchi company, who had to confront a difficult situation when he began his activity in 1885. Before the introduction of the safety bicycle, the image of cycling evoked something hilarious, unsafe, awkward and tangled. It was clear that legitimizing bicycle use was a key issue that any bicycle firm could not ignore if it was to succeed. As a result, it was necessary to face the public's aversion to bicycles induced by previous nineteenth century attempts to develop the machine. The best way to change attitudes towards cycling, and popularize the new practice of individual mobility was to demonstrate the technical improvements that had given birth to the safety bicycle. If people could see the bicycle in action, they would grasp how different was the new design and how the problems of earlier designs were solved. The opportunity of showing people cycling in action was offered by the nascent bicycle road races that took place across many countries, particularly in Europe. These road races provide millions of people with their initial exposure to the first modern spectator sport. Riders passed by their homes and local communities and spectators were able to participate directly in the races without the need for tickets or travel to distant sport venues. Bicycles were the essential tool of this newly popularized sport and road races became the springboard to boosting the bicycle's use by showing it in action (Mari 2015, p. 149). The stage offered by road races helped bicycle firms to overcome the aversion to bicycles, which in turn increased the practice of cycling, which ultimately affected favourably the sales of bicycles. Despite the fact that competitive cycling was something different to using bicycles for transportation or leisure purposes, the impact of marketing through sports was beneficial to the entire activity of cycling as these further uses of the bicycle were not mutually exclusive, and interchange between then frequently occurred. For instance, the same individual might race on the weekend, and ride to work during the week (Ritchie 2018, p. 9).

A further reason that explains the relationship between the bicycle industry and the sports is that races were the primary testing ground for bicycle technology. The real racing environment became the best way to test products and innovations that were, subsequently, transferred to the production of bicycles. It is fair to say that there was a mutually beneficial relationship between bicycle racing and the industry. The sports asked the industry for advanced machines characterized by lightness and speed, and the industry needed racing for improving its products through innovation and technical changes.

The relationship between bicycle racing and the industry can be better understood through the archetype of competitive cycling exemplified by stage-races on the road, particularly the two most celebrated and long-lived races mentioned earlier: the Tour de France and the Giro d'Italia. The Tour borrowed the idea of racing in stages from motor sport, such as cars and motorcycles, which had been developing this kind of event for several years (Dauncey 2012, p. 85). For instance, in 1901 it was organized a successful automobile tour of Italy (Mari 2015, p. 150). In turn, the formula of the Tour inspired other European countries to introduce their own national tours: the Tour of Belgium in 1908, the Tour of Holland in 1909, the Giro d'Italia in 1909, the Tour of Germany in 1911 and the Tour of Catalonia in 1911 (Ritchie 2018, p. 272).

The Tour was invented by the French newspaper *L'Auto-Vélo*, launched in October 1900, as a means to compete against its main rival *Le Vélo*. The founding commercial premise was clear: the race could act as a way to sell more newspapers to the public and advertising space to the bicycle industry, both in the pages of *L'Auto-Vélo* and on the backs and bikes of riders (Dauncey 2012, p. 110). The formula of the Tour was developed according to the needs of the newspaper to maximize its sales. A race divided into stages facilitated reporting, and allowed a style of journalism based on anecdote and fostered a sense of the evolving drama of the competition. The commentary by journalists was made before, during, and after the long stages, and the fact that stages were separated by periods of rests allowed further opportunities to sell copy covering further topics not directly related to racing. Moreover, the organization of start times and distances of stages facilitated printing deadlines and maximizing crowds at the finish lines (Dauncey 2012, p. 85). The Tour was since its very beginning a for-profit event, it became the commercial linkage between the sporting press and the bicycle industry. Both worked together to shape the Tour into an entertainment spectacle. Bicycle firms sponsored teams of professional cyclists to compete in the Tour, assuming that the success of their team in races would have generated more free press coverage (that is, more newspaper articles and pictures generated in the press coverage of racing) that could have been realized with the same amount of directly purchased advertising (Brewer 2002, p. 292). In 1931, the Tour further emphasized its for-profit nature by opening the event to businesses outside the bicycle industry, known as *extra-sportifs*, seeking to use the spectacle of the Tour to promote their products (Reed 2003, p. 105). The evolution of this event highlights the nexus of relations between sports, media, and bicycle industry that would have become even more intertwined in the television age during the 1960s.

The Giro d'Italia shares many analogies with the Tour. It was invented by the biweekly magazine *Gazzetta dello Sport*, founded in 1896, particularly focused on road cycling races. This magazine began to organize its own races as a way to overcome the increasing competition from other sports magazines. In 1905, it started the first Giro della Lombardia and two years later the first Milan-Sanremo, in 1907. It announced that the first Italian cycling tour was ready for starting in 1909 to pre-empt a similar plan from the *Corriere della Sera*, a leading Italian newspaper, which was trying to organize a road race across the country similar to the Tour (Mari 2015, p. 150). The race was a great success and, as a result, the *Gazzetta dello Sport* became a triweekly magazine in 1909 and a daily newspaper in 1913. The Giro d'Italia opened the event to businesses outside the bicycle industry in 1954, and the nexus of relations with the media became stronger with the advent of television in the second half of the 1950s. The Giro d'Italia was held every year since the 1909 edition, except during the 1915–1918 and 1940–1945 time frame for world wars.

The data available, regarding the first 94 editions from 1909 to 2011 (Castellano 2012), provide a snapshot of the participation of the bicycle industry to this road race. A note of caution is needed in examining these data as it was not always possible to clearly discern the names of bicycle firms and, as a result, some assumptions were made. Moreover, the category of bicycle firms only includes manufacturers of bicycles and tyres. The first long phase of the participation of the bicycle industry to the Giro d'Italia lasted for about 45 years from 1909 to 1954 (Fig. 3.4).

Data show that the total number of racing teams is almost overlapped with the number of bicycle firms sponsoring their own racing team. Until 1934 there was a synergy between bicycle manufacturers and tyre manufactures as most teams were a jointly endeavour of these firms. For instance, Alcyon and Hutchinson, Atala and Continental, Bianchi and

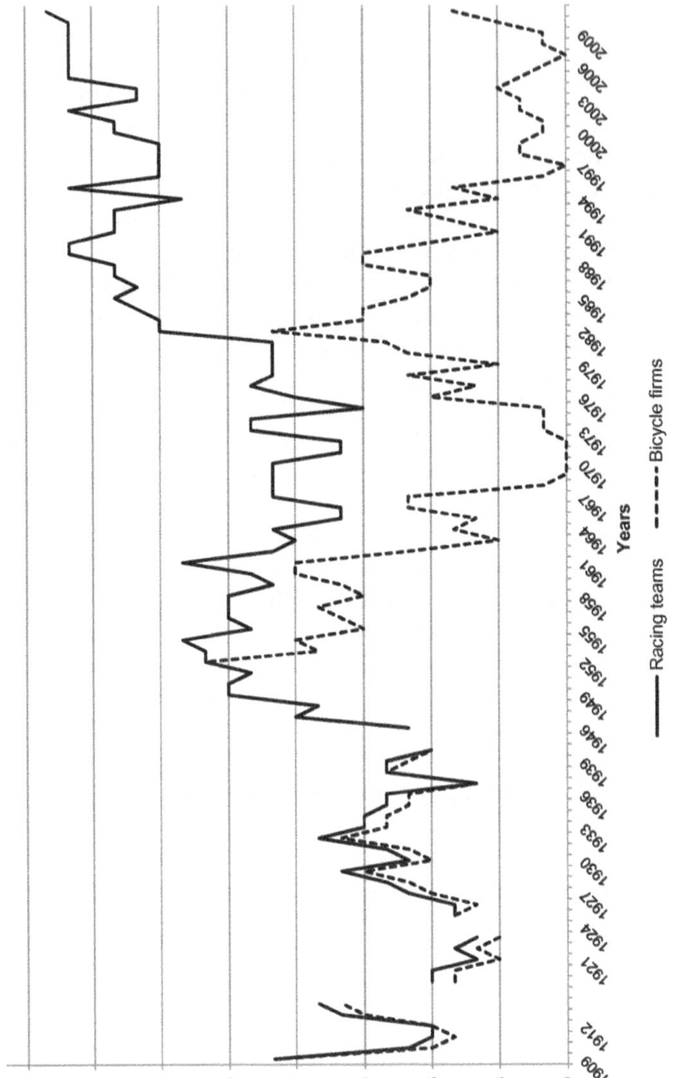

Fig. 3.4 Racing teams at Giro d'Italia in 1909–2011

Pirelli, Legnano and Dunlop. After 1934 the tyres manufacturers abandoned the Giro d'Italia and returned to participate from 1951 to 1962, not on a regular basis. The mid-1950s saw a significant decrease of racing teams emanating from bicycle firms. This reduction was even worst during the 1962–1975 time frame when bicycle firms almost disappeared from the Giro d'Italia. They were substituted by other companies outside the bicycle industry. From the mid-1970s to 1982 bicycle firms joined again the Giro d'Italia and afterwards a long series of fluctuations until 2011, which could be interpreted as dictated by contingent decisions by bicycle firms. The year 1954 is the watershed of the contribution of bicycle firms to the Giro d'Italia and almost matches the end of the so-called golden age of the Italian competitive cycling. It is clear, from the data available, that after 1954 an increasing number of companies outside the bicycle industry were using road races as a marketing tool. This situation in Italy mirrored what happened across Europe and elsewhere. A partial explanation of the continuous exit of bicycle firms from the Giro d'Italia is the cost involved in sponsoring a racing team. According to some estimates (Van Reeth 2016, p. 57), the yearly average total budget of the ten best performing road racing teams jumped from approximately 4 million euro in 1992 to almost 14 million euro in 2004. A further source (Desbordes 2006, pp. 407–408) provide estimates about the total budget of 30 professional cycling teams registered with the Union Cycliste Internationale (UCI). In 2003, the annual budget ranged from 1.5 to 8 million euro, and, in 2004, from 1.5 to 12 million euro.

It would be useful to understand whether the introduction of off-road races, since the 1980s, impacted the choice of bicycle firms to invest money in competitive cycling. Data about mountain bike racing are not available and it is not possible to provide any evidence, however, it seems plausible to argue that bicycle firms, particularly small and medium-sized enterprises, had difficulties to participate, in the same sport season, to both road and off-road racing.

3.5 Conclusion

Marketing in the bicycle industry has not changed after many years. Bicycle firms seem to suffer from structural inertia, which makes them unable to adapt to internal and external challenges. Internal factors, such as routines and traditions, and external forces, such as competitive pressures and access to resources, determine strong inertial pressures on structure, which, in turn, make organizational change extremely difficult to accomplish (Suddaby and Foster 2017, p. 22). Should bicycle marketing change? Someone might argue that there is no need to change, if it has somehow worked until today why worrying about changing it. There are at least three reasons that suggest thinking about changes in practising bicycle marketing. Each of them is associated with one of the three pillars examined earlier.

Bicycle firms still try to understand their potential customers using the market segmentation framework developed more than 100 years ago. After such a long time, it is useful to ask if this is the most suitable approach for gaining enough knowledge about customers. Perhaps a more advanced framework, based on gathering primary data directly into the market, would provide valuable insights, which could lead to develop an offering closer to customer needs and wants.

The practice of annual collection is considered the right path to introduce innovation and improvements into the market since the nineteenth century, but there is also an alternative view that sees it as a wasteful manipulation of the consumer. Moreover, annual model change puts a tremendous pressure on the manufacturing process and marketing activity of any bicycle firm. It is time that the bicycle industry thinks about a different way of doing business, staring from lengthening the life cycle of its offerings.

Some preliminary data about the participation of bicycle firms to road races show that bicycle industry is perhaps rethinking its relationship with sports as a marketing tool. If it is true, the bicycle industry could consider to broaden its role and provide a contribution to a more sustainable mobility, particularly urban mobility. City cycling might be a valuable opportunity for bicycle firms truly committed to offer their support for changing the urban transportation system.

References

Aronson, S. H. (1952). The sociology of the bicycle. *Social Forces, 30*(3), 305–312.

Brewer, B. D. (2002). Commercialization in professional cycling 1950–2001: Institutional transformations and the rationalization of "doping". *Sociology of Sport Journal, 19*, 276–301.

Castellano, C. (2012). *Giro d'Italia: 1909–2011. History and statistics*. Milan, Italy: RCS Sport.

Chandler, A. D., Jr. (Ed.). (1964). *Giant enterprise: Ford, General Motors, and the automobile industry. Sources and readings*. New York, NY: Harcourt, Brace & World, Inc.
Church, R. (1982). Markets and marketing in the British motor industry before 1914 with some French comparisons. *The Journal of Transport History, 3*(1), 1–20.
Cohen, L. (1990). The mass in mass consumption. *Reviews in American History, 18*(4), 548–555.
Dauncey, H. (2012). *French cycling. A social and cultural history*. Liverpool, UK: Liverpool University Press.
Desbordes, M. (2006). The economics of cycling. In W. Andreff & S. Szymanski (Eds.), *Handbook on the economics of sport* (pp. 55–82). Cheltenham, UK: Edward Elgar Publishing Limited.
Dowell, G. (2006). Product line strategies of new entrants in an established industry: Evidence from the U.S. bicycle industry. *Strategic Management Journal, 27*, 959–979.
Duncans, H. O. (1898). The cycle industry. *The Contemporary Review, 73*, 500–511.
Fullerton, R. A. (1988). How modern is modern marketing? Marketing's evolution and the myth of the "production era". *Journal of Marketing, 52*(January), 108–125.
Fullerton, R. A. (2016). Segmentation in practice. An historical overview of the eighteenth and nineteenth centuries. In B. D. G. Jones & M. Tadajewski (Eds.), *The Routledge companion to marketing history* (pp. 85–95). Abingdon, UK: Routledge.
Giant. (2010a). *Full line catalog 2011*. Taichung City, Taiwan: Giant Manufacturing Co., Ltd.
Giant. (2010b). *Price list 2011*. Taichung City, Taiwan: Giant Manufacturing Co., Ltd.
Harrison, A. E. (1977). *Growth, entrepreneurship and capital formation in the United Kindom's cycle and related industries, 1870–1914*. PhD thesis, University of York.
Hounshell, D. A. (1979). The bicycle and technology in late nineteenth century America. In P. Sörbom (Ed.), *Tecniska Museet Symposia: Transport technology and social change* (pp. 172–185). Stockholm, Sweden: Tecniska Museet.
Hounshell, D. A. (1984). *From the American system to mass production 1800–1932. The development of manufacturing technology in the United States*. Baltimore, MD: The Johns Hopkins University Press.
Lee Blaszczyk, R. (2000). *Imagining consumers. Design and innovation from Wedgwood to Corning*. Baltimore, MD: The Johns Hopkins University Press.
Mari, C. (2015). Putting the Italians on bicycles: Marketing at Bianchi, 1885–1955. *Journal of Historical Research in Marketing, 7*(1), 133–158.

McKendrick, N. (1982). Josiah Wedgwood and the commercialization of potteries. In N. McKendrick, J. Brewer, & J. H. Plumb (Eds.), *The birth of a consumer society. The commercialization of eighteenth-century England* (pp. 100–145). London, UK: Europa Publications Limited.

Millward, A. (1999). *Factors contributing to the sustained success of the UK cycle industry 1870–1939*. PhD thesis, University of Birmingham.

Oliver, S. H., & Berkebile, D. H. (1974). *Wheels and wheeling. The Smithsonian cycle collection*. Washington, DC: Smithsonian Institution Press.

Petty, R. D. (1995). Peddling the bicycle in the 1890s: Mass marketing shifts into high gear. *Journal of Macromarketing*, Spring, 32–46.

Reed, E. (2003). The economics of the tour 1930–2003. *International Journal of the History of Sport, 20*(2), 103–127.

Ritchie, A. (2018). *Early bicycles and the quest for speed. A history, 1868–1903* (2nd ed.). Jefferson, NC: McFarland & Company Inc.

Roseo, G. G. (1912). *L'industria e il commercio dei velocipedi nel mondo*. Milan, Italy: Libreria Editrice Milanese.

Rothschild, E. (1973). *Paradise lost. The decline of the auto-industrial age*. New York, NY: Random House.

Rover Cycle Company Limited. (1897). *Catalogue and price list 1898*. Coventry, UK: Rover Cycle Company Limited.

Sachs, W. (1992). *For love of the automobile. Looking back into the history of our desires*. Berkeley, CA: University of California Press.

Sanderson, S. W., & Uzumeri, M. (1997). *Managing product families*. Chicago, IL: Irwin.

Sheller, M., & Urry, J. (2000). The city and the car. *International Journal of Urban and Regional Research, 24*(4), 737–757.

Sloan, A. P., Jr. (1990 [1963]). *My years with general motors*. New York, NY: Doubleday Currency.

Suddaby, R., & Foster, W. M. (2017). History and organizational change. *Journal of Management, 43*(1), 19–38.

Tedlow, R. S. (1990). *New and improved. The story of mass marketing in America*. New York, NY: Basic Books Inc.

Tedlow, R. S. (2015). The fourth phase of marketing. Marketing history and the business world today. In R. S. Tedlow & G. Jones (Eds.), *The rise and fall of mass marketing* (pp. 8–35). Abingdon, UK: Routledge.

Tedlow, R. S., & Jones, G. (2015). Introduction. In R. S. Tedlow & G. Jones (Eds.), *The rise and fall of mass marketing* (pp. 1–7). Abingdon, UK: Routledge.

The Raleigh Cycle Co. Ltd. (1889). *Catalogue and price list season 1890*. Nottingham, UK: The Raleigh Cycle Co. Ltd.

The Raleigh Cycle Co. Ltd. (1906). *Catalogue and price list season 1907*. Nottingham, UK: The Raleigh Cycle Co. Ltd.

Trentmann, F. (2017). *Empire of things. How we became a world of consumers, form the 15th century to the 21st*. London, UK: Penguin Books.
Ulrich, K. T. (2005). *Design. Creation of artifacts in society*. Philadelphia, PA: University of Pennsylvania.
Van Reeth, D. (2016). The finances of professional cycling teams. In D. Van Reeth & D. J. Larson (Eds.), *The economics of professional road cycling* (pp. 55–82). Cham, Switzerland: Springer International Publishing.

CHAPTER 4

Twenty Years of Marketing in the Italian Bicycle Market: Cannondale 1998–2017

Abstract This chapter is focuses on the experience of a well-known bicycle firm and its marketing activity. The analysis deals with its product policy decisions in a specific European market over a twenty years time. The company, named Cannondale, provides a significant example for understanding the complex marketing process carried out by this firm and many others in the bicycle industry. The chapter includes a preliminary historical background to get familiar with the firm. Further sections discuss the market offering of Cannondale and how it evolved over time. Specifically, how the company created and managed variety in its product lines, and which dimensions of variety were employed.

Keywords Fit variety · Taste variety · Quality variety · Catalogue · Price list · Price tier

4.1 A Short History of Cannondale Corporation

The previous chapter examined the fundamental nature of marketing practice in the bicycle industry and laid the basis for understanding the marketing strategy of a particular bicycle firm over a long period of time. The focus is on analysing the offering of a foreign firm in the Italian bicycle market using the data of a 20-year time series drawn from the catalogues and price lists covering the 1998–2017 time frame. These data

C. Mari, *A Business History of the Bicycle Industry*,
https://doi.org/10.1007/978-3-030-50563-9_4

allow to provide a thorough examination of two marketing pillars, out of three, presented earlier: market segmentation and market offering.

The bicycle firm considered in this chapter is Cannondale Corporation, a well-known brand of bicycles founded in the United States by Joseph Montgomery in the early 1970s. The year of its inception is 1970 or 1971, depending on which version of the story is recalled. The company catalogues of 1973, 1983, and 1989 tell that in the early winter of 1970, or in the late summer of 1970, the business was started in a space close to the rail station of Wilton in Connecticut, and the name of the company was chosen by chance looking at the train station's sign, which was Cannondale (Cannondale Corporation 1973, 1983, 1988). The catalogue of 1996 recalls the same story, but this time the year is 1971 (Cannondale Corporation 1995). Perhaps the explanation is simply that a fiscal year was considered rather than a calendar year. For the sake of clarity, it should be highlighted that bicycle firms usually publish their catalogues and price lists, every year, in the autumn of the preceding year. In other words the catalogue of the 1989 season is available approximately in September or October of 1988. At the same time, it is plausible to argue that the catalogues of Cannondale before 1984 do not necessarily follow this practice, since the offering of the company did not include bicycles yet.

Cannondale corporation started as a manufacturer of backpacking and bicycling equipment, such as packs, and bikepack touring system (that is, handlebar pack, seat pack and rear rack pack). Through the 1970s and early 1980s, the company became known for an expanding line of quality bike camping equipment. For instance, a mini-trailer that bike campers could use to tow their gear, a bicycle carrier, a tent, a sleeping bag and a security chain and lock. It was also added a line of apparel, such as insulated clothing, jerseys, shorts, T-shirts and caps. The experience gained through this kind of offering was crucial for Cannondale, particularly to develop a distribution channel capability and, at the same time, build its brand identity (Stone 1998, p. 509). In 1982 the founder of Cannondale met David Graham, an engineer, and they agreed to build an aluminium bicycle, which came out in 1983. This was the first key diversification of Cannondale's business, and it was a very successful choice for the company. The first bicycle was presented as ideal for long distance touring, time trailing, and everything in-between. Cannondale built the frame using large diameter aluminium alloy to make the bicycle structurally stiffer. The unusually fat tubing gave it a distinctive look. All the fabrication equipment for the aluminium frame had to be custom designed and it was difficult to obtain components that would fit this kind of frame. All components were supplied by third parties. In a few years, Cannondale saw sales explode and expanded its offering adding new models, such as racing bicycles, all-terrain bicycles (later called mountain bicycles), town and country bicycles and tandem bicycles. The company continuously grew in the domestic market and abroad. In 1989, it established a European subsidiary in the Netherlands, which imported components and bicycle frames made in the United States and assembled them. In fiscal year 1992, it began operations in Japan through its subsidiary, which imported fully assembled bicycles, and in 1996 it was formed Cannondale Australia, which imported fully assembled bicycles (Cannondale Corporation 2002a). Cannondale's headquarters was in Bethel (in Connecticut), and its production facilities were located in Bedford (in Pennsylvania), for bicycles and clothing, and in Phillipsburg (in Pennsylvania), for accessories, some clothing, and bicycles subassemblies. In 2001, it employed 773 full-time employees in the United States, 130 in Europe, 14 in Japan, and 6 in Australia (Cannondale Corporation 2002a).

Cannondale put its effort into developing hand-welded aluminium bicycle frames through an innovative production process based on a flexible manufacturing system, patented in 1993. A process employed lasers and other devices to cut the uniquely configured joints of various bicycle models without individual setup or changeover. A slot-and-tub approach allowed parts to interlock without special tools to hold tubes in place for welding. The whole system enabled the cost effective production of a wide offering and a broad range of models in a single day in order to respond to consumer demand. The average time to complete a bicycle fell down from 17 to 3 days (Cannondale Corporation 1995; Stone 1998, p. 505; Ulrich et al. 1998, p. 186). The bicycle frame was the pivotal feature of any bicycle made by Cannondale, and each frame was marketed carrying a *Handmade in USA* logo.

The company changed its business system in 1992 when decided to start the manufacturing of some components, such as handlebars, bar-ends, seat binders, grips, brakes, hubs and cranksets. Cannondale developed a proprietary line of components under the CODA (Cannondale Original Design Application) brand, which appeared for the first time in the 1993 catalogue (Cannondale Corporation 1992). The brand CODA was used until 1999 as shown in the 2000 catalogue (Cannondale

Corporation 1999a). Afterwards, Cannondale disused it, even though it continued to manufacture some components, which were indicated as Cannondale components in the catalogues. Until 1991, almost all components were supplied by third parties, whereas in 1996, 20% were Cannondale components (Stone 1998, p. 510). The company extensively relied on sports as a marketing tool and also as a testing ground for its technological innovations. In 1994, it sponsored a mountain bike racing team, and since 1997 a professional road racing team. It was also involved in sponsoring a triathlon racing team and many individual athletes.

In November 1994, Cannondale went public, offering 2,300,000 shares of common stock. The founder of the company owned 30.2% of the company stock, and company employees owned another 15% (Stone 1998, pp. 511–512). The year 2000 was a watershed for Cannondale since it decided its second diversification. The growth strategy was based on entering the motorsports market with the production of a motocross motorcycle for off-road racing purposes, and two four-wheeled all-terrain vehicles (ATVs). In May 2000, it launched the first motorcycle, and between February and June 2001, the two ATVs. The plan was to manufacture and sell a total of eight 2002 model year motorsports products: four motorcycles and four ATVs (Cannondale Corporation 2002a). The strategy did not work due to a continuing cash drain associated with the new business and, on January 27th of 2003, Cannondale announced its plan to file to restructure the company under Chapter 11 of the Bankruptcy Code, as the founder explained in his letter to Cannondale's customers (Montgomery 2003). Figure 4.1 shows the revenues and operating income of both businesses, and it was clear that the motorsports diversification was compromising the core business of the company.

The restructuring was seen as the most suitable way to preserve and strengthen the bicycle business. Cannondale concluded the Chapter 11 process in May 2003 with the closing on the sales of the assets of its bicycle and motorsports divisions to affiliates of Pegasus Partners II, L.P., a private equity investment firm based in Connecticut. The bicycle business remained profitable, despite the burden and distraction that the motorsports division imposed, and was incorporated as the Cannondale Bicycle Corporation. Pegasus planned to sell the motorsports division (Hartford 2003), and implemented some changes in managing Cannondale, which included several job cuts and outsourcing apparel manufacturing. In the summer of 2005, Cannondale acquired Sugoi Performance Apparel, a Canadian firm of apparel for cycling, training, and

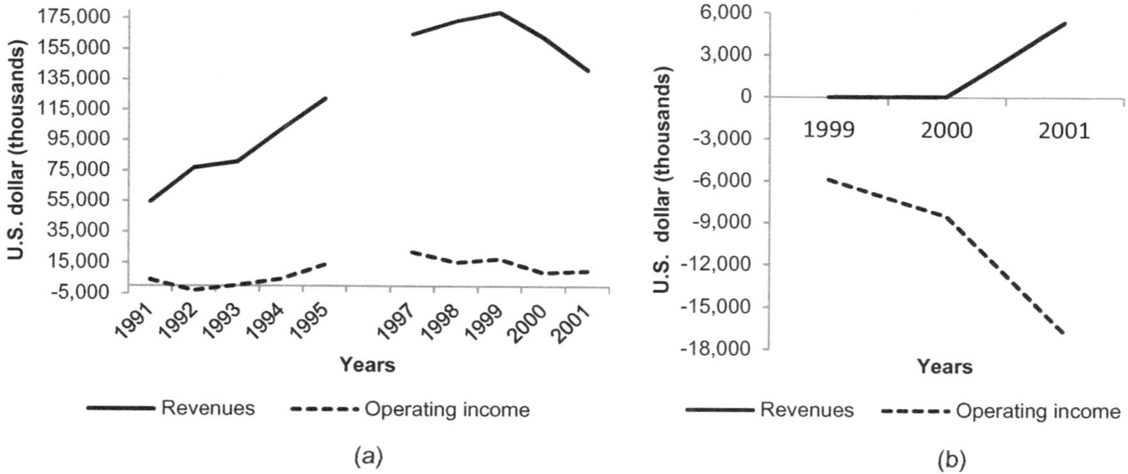

Fig. 4.1 Cannondale revenues and operating income **a** Bicycle business 1991–2001 and **b** Motorsports business 1999–2001

triathlon. In February 2008, after owning Cannondale for less than five years, Pegasus sold the company (including Sugoi) to Dorel Industries, a publicly listed Montreal based company (Norman 2008).

Dorel was established in 1962 and its activity is organized into three areas of businesses: Juvenile Products (such as infant car seats, strollers, high chairs, toddler beds, playpens, swings and infants health and safety aids), Recreational/Leisure (such as bicycles, jogging strollers, scooters and other recreational products), and Home Furnishings (such as ready-to-assemble furniture, metal folding furniture, step stools and ladders). Dorel entered the bicycle industry in 2004 through the acquisition of Pacific Cycle, the owner of Schwinn, Mongoose and GT Bicycle brands. After the acquisition of Cannondale, Dorel created a new division, named Cannondale Sports Group, within the company's Recreational/Leisure business. As a result, Pacific Cycle became a stand-alone division with an exclusive focus on mass merchant customers, and Cannondale Sports Group, including Sugoi and GT Bicycles, was committed to the independent bicycle dealer channel (Dorel Industries Inc. 2008). In 2009, Cannondale Sports Group was renamed as Cycling Sports Group, and the recreational/leisure was reorganized around three primary divisions: Cycling Sports Group (CSG), Pacific Cycle and Apparel Footwear Group. During the same year, Dorel decided to consolidate all North American product development, marketing, and business management functions for all four cycling brands (Cannondale, Schwinn, GT and Mongoose) to Bethel in Connecticut, within the Cycling Sports Group. Moreover, it was created a bicycle testing laboratory at the other location of Cannondale in Bedford, in Pennsylvania (Dorel Industries Inc. 2010, 2011). This choice meant that Cannondale was no longer a bicycle frame manufacturer, and 2009 was the last year to see a bicycle frame carrying a *Handmade in USA* logo. The production moved to Asia in 2010, and Dorel established a sourcing operation in Taiwan to oversee the Far East supplier base and logistics chain, to ensure that its products are manufactured to meet the quality standards required. The process of restructuring continued and, in 2013, the Recreational/Leisure business changed name into Dorel Sports. It was also decided to close the bicycle testing laboratory in Bedford, and to relocate the activity carried out in Bethel to the new headquarters in Wilton, in Connecticut, and, at the same time, to sell the building facilities in Bethel. In 2019, the European operations of Cycling Sports Group were centralized in the Netherlands at the

Cannondale facility in Oldenzaal. The existing assembly plant was transformed to increase its production capacity of Cannondale bicycles and electric-bicycles. The office portion of the Oldenzaal facility was closed.

The annual reports of Dorel include aggregate data for each business and, consequently, it is not possible to know any specific information about Cannondale, such as revenues, operating income, number of employees, or number of bicycle assembled and sold. There are some data about the use of sports as a marketing tool. For instance, in 2009, Dorel provided Cannondale bicycles to a professional road racing team, and from 2010 to 2011, it was a co-sponsor of a road racing team. From 2012 through 2017, it fully sponsored a professional road racing team, named Cannondale Pro Cycling Team (Dorel Industries Inc. 2010, 2011, 2012, 2013, 2014, 2015, 2016, 2017, 2018, 2019, 2020).

In about ten years, Cannondale has become something very different from what it was. Cannondale began its activity, in the bicycle industry, as a frame maker from 1983 to 1991. One year later, in 1992, it changed its business system adding some components manufacturing and it became a vertically integrated firm. This situation lasted until 2009, when the new owner of Cannondale decided to discontinue the production of bicycle frames and components. In 2010, Cannondale changed again its business system to become an assembler and this decision marked the end of one of the very few US bicycle frame makers.

4.2 Cannondale's Market Offering

This section examines the market offering of Cannondale in Europe, particularly the Italian market, using a time series of twenty years, starting from 1998 up to 2017. The analysis is based on data drawn from two company sources: catalogue and price list of each year. For sake of conciseness, both sources are included in the reference section and not cited throughout this section. It was not possible to find the same documents, particularly the price list, for further years before and after the 1998–2017 time frame. The time series provides enough information to discuss and trace the evolution of how Cannondale developed its market offering for the Italian market, during a twenty-year time frame. Consistent with the analysis developed in the previous chapter, the main variables used to understand the offering of Cannondale are as follows: the number of product lines, the number of models, the number of product variants, the number of bicycle frames, and the three categories of variety (that is, fit, taste, and quality).

Cannondale's product policy was extensively based on the annual model change approach. Every year the whole offering was changed. In some cases the company introduced genuine innovations, such as the suspension system for both front and rear wheel, in many other cases, the changes were simply cosmetic, such as the name of a model or the introduction of a new colour. Over time, catalogues show how valuable changes coexist with fashion and fad that duly appear every year. According to the annual model change, Cannondale continuously modified its product lines of high-performance bicycles for the adult market, sold through the specialty bicycle retail channel. In 1998, its offering was organized into five product lines: road and multisport, touring, commuters, hybrids, mountain, and tandems. These categories were based on bicycle usage and some technical features of bicycles as well. For instance, they included bicycles used for competitions, for triathlons, or cyclo-cross; bicycles for travelling; bicycles for city cycling; bicycles for around town cruising; bicycles for off-road riding; and bicycles built-for-two. Cannondale changed its product lines over time, but it is not clear whether such modifications were rooted into a sound market analysis, or simply resulted from a contingency approach aimed at seizing on a market opportunity. Product lines were easily added in a season and discontinued the next year. In some cases, it seemed that Cannondale tried to appeal to potential customers through an offering based on a lifestyle market segmentation. Some catalogues and price lists presented product lines through names that could evoke bicycle usage as a way of sharing a particular lifestyle. A partial list of these name includes: bad boy, road warrior, hooligan, freeride, marathon, adventure, easy rider, comfort or fitness.

When looking at the whole picture, it is fair to state that the entire offering was organized around three product lines, which encompassed the variety of models developed by Cannondale. They can be categorized as follows: mountain bicycles, road and multisport bicycles, urban and leisure bicycles. This offering was changed during the 1998–2017 time frame in three ways.

Firstly, the company strengthened its offering of models specifically designed for women. The catalogues and price lists show that some urban and recreational bicycles for women were already available since 1998, however, only later, in 2001, it was launched a road and multisport line named *feminine*. In 2002, it was added a mountain line for women, and until 2017, the offering for this group of potential customers significantly increased through a variety of models covering the three product lines mentioned earlier. Secondly, Cannondale launched a product line for children in 2013, in Europe, and one year later in Italy. This was a notable change in the company strategy, which was exclusively committed to serve the adult market since its foundation. Instead, Dorel Industries was already involved in providing bicycles to children market before the acquisition of Cannondale. Thirdly, in 2012 Cannondale added an electric bicycle product line to address the increasing demand for this category of bicycles. Figure 4.2 depicts a comparison between the number of models included in each product line from 1998 to 2017.

The entire offering significantly expanded its variety, from 68 models in 1998 up to 227 in 2017. It is clear that mountain, road, and urban product lines were the core offering of Cannondale for twenty years. The share of mountain bicycle models ranged between 30 and 44% every year, and it was 34% since 2016. There were 30 models in 1998 and 78 in 2017, with a yearly average of approximately 40 models. The share of road bicycle models ranged between 25 and 39%, and it was 30% since 2016. In 1998, there were 17 models and, in 2017, 69 models, with a yearly average of approximately 37 models. The share of urban bicycle models ranged between 25 and 33% during the 1998–2012 time frame. Between 2013 and 2017 it dropped to 15%. There were 18 models in 1998 and 34 in 2017, with a yearly average of 30 models. Tandem models were a minor share within the offering, ranging between 5 and 7% from 1998 to 2003. Then, it became a share of approximately 2–3%, and 1% since 2015. In 2012 and 2013 tandems were not available in the Italian market. The share of electric bicycle models grew very rapidly since 2012 and reached 15% in 2017. There were 4 models in 2012 and 33 in 2017. Children bicycle models accounted for approximately 5% of the offering.

Figure 4.3 provides a further perspective on the entire offering during the twenty years. This time, data regarding each product line are omitted to provide a broader focus on models, product variants, and bicycle frames.

It can be clearly seen that there was a relationship linking together models and bicycle frames. Over time, the more models were added, the more bicycle frame were needed. The yearly average number of models per bicycle frame was approximately 3. It meant that Cannondale was able to use a single bicycle frame for three models across its various product

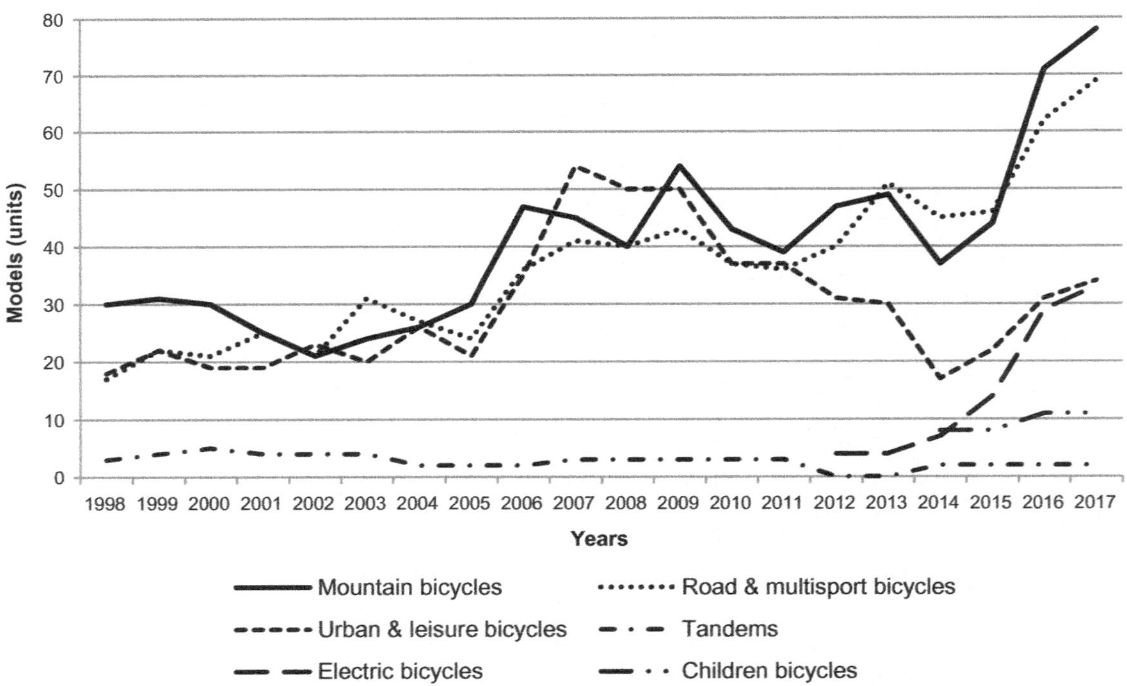

Fig. 4.2 Models and product lines 1998–2017

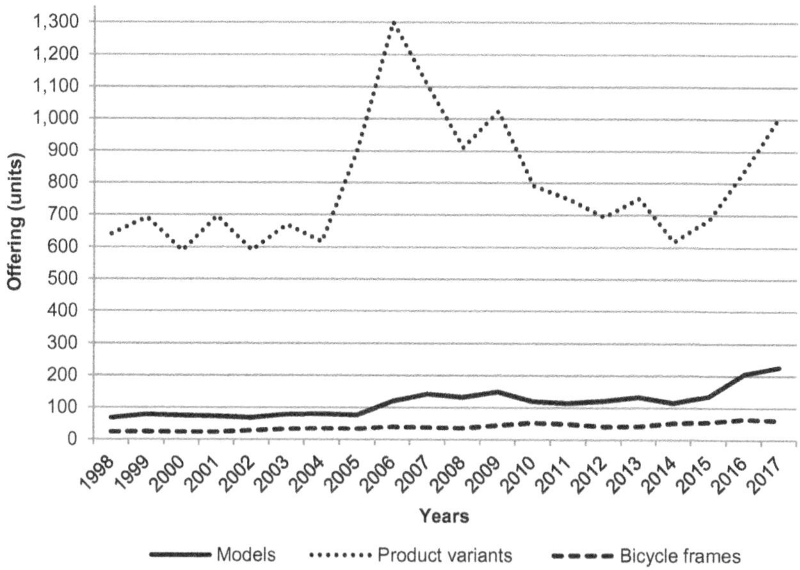

Fig. 4.3 Models, product variants, and bicycle frames 1998–2017

lines. There were 23 bicycle frames in 1998 and 62 in 2017. The other evident information was the continuous fluctuations of product variants, which depended on bicycle size, bicycle colour, and potential options. Changing one of this dimension could produce a significant impact on the number of product variants, and it was usually the fastest way to modify the offering. There was a total of 641 product variants in 1998 and 1011 in 2017. The trend, since 1998, was to reduce the average number of product variants per model. It ranged between 8 and 12 product variants, from 1998 to 2007. It dropped to 7 product variants during the 2008–2011 time frame. It continued to fall and reached 6 product variants in 2012–2013, then 5 product variants in 2014–2015, and lastly 4 product variants in 2016–2017.

The next section examines the three main product lines of Cannondale, particularly how variety was created and managed over time in each of them. The other three product lines are not discussed further. As already mentioned, tandem product line was a minor activity for Cannondale and it was also a special category of bicycle. Children product line is a recent addition to the offering and was beyond the scope of its marketing strategy for most of the twenty years. Electric bicycles were the rising product line but they played a minor role during the 1998–2017 time frame. It is plausible that, in the near future, this product line will become a key resource for the bicycle industry.

4.3 Dimensions of Variety at Cannondale

The focus of this section is on the three key product lines of Cannondale, analysed through the categories of fit, taste, and quality variety. The data drawn from catalogues and price lists provide a first overview of each product line highlighting the number of models, the number of product variants and the number of bicycle frames. Mountain and road product lines increased their number of models and of bicycle frames during the twenty years (Fig. 4.4). Urban product line showed a different pattern: a growth in the number of models and more variations in the number of bicycle frames. The average number of mountain product variants per model was 7, from 1998 to 2011, then dropped to 5 in 2012 and continued to decline to 4 in 2013 through 2017. The average number of mountain bicycle frames per model was 3, from 1998 to 2007, then increased to 4 in 2008 and remained steady until 2017. Road and multisport product line showed a similar trend. The average number of product variants per model was 14, from 1998 to 2010, then began a persistent reduction to 9 in 2011–2013, to 8 in 2014–2015 and to 6 in 2016–2017. The average number of bicycle frame per model increased from 3, in 1998–2007, to 5 in 2008–2017. Urban and leisure product line also showed a reduction in the average number of product variants per model from 6, in 1998–2007, to 4, in 2008–2017. Its average number of bicycle frame per model was 3 during the twenty years. Overall, it seems clear that Cannondale was trying to prune its offering through a joint action based on the reduction of the average number of product variants per model, and the increase of the average number of bicycle frame per model. Figure 4.4 also makes evident the continuous fluctuations in the number of product variants of each product line. As discussed earlier, it is possible to speculate that such a variation stems from contingent decisions rather than a sound marketing strategy.

The analysis of each product line can be further extended through the three types of variety introduced in the previous chapter. The discussion is therefore intended to answer the following question: How did Cannondale carry out fit, taste, and quality variety between 1998 and 2017? Fit

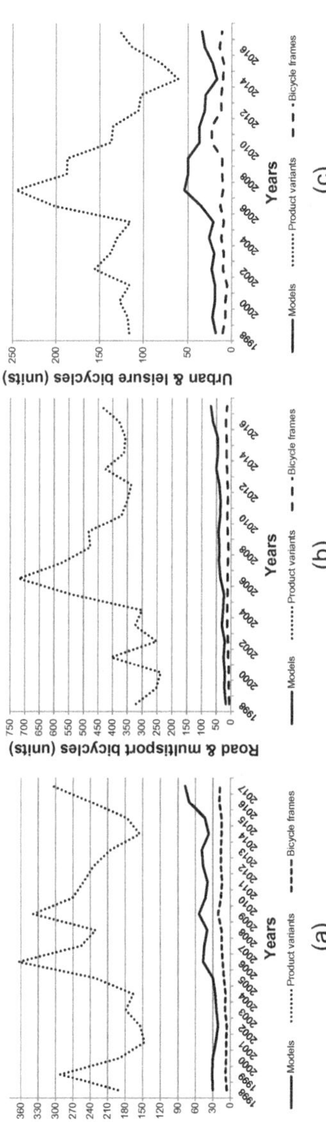

Fig. 4.4 Offering 1998–2017 **a** Mountain bicycles, **b** Road & multisport bicycles, and **c** Urban & leisure bicycles

variety is related to anthropometric measures and Cannondale employed two bicycle features for making its offering closer to customer needs and wants. Firstly, and most importantly, it designed its bicycle frames in different sizes according to basic human body measurements and frame geometry. The latter refers to all the angles and tube lengths, which affect the handling and riding qualities of a bicycle. Frame geometry depends on the use for which a bicycle is designed. It means that mountain, road, and urban bicycles have different frame geometry. Ideally, a bicycle firm should manufacture highly individual bicycle frames, which perfectly fit the anthropometric measures of every individual customer. Such a customized approach is rarely viable and, as a result, bicycle firms make a trade-off between the needs of potential customers and their goals. Pragmatically, this means to decide how many bicycle frame sizes have to be designed and manufactured for each model included within the offering.

The catalogues and price lists of Cannondale, from 1998 to 2017, enable to compare the number of bicycle frame sizes of mountain, road and multisport, and urban and leisure product lines. Figure 4.5 summarizes some key data highlighting the lowest and highest number of bicycle frame sizes available for each product line, during the twenty years. There are variations within and among product lines. Overall, it can be stated that most of the mountain bicycle models were proposed to the market in 4–5 frame sizes every year. Exceptions to this practice were justified for special cases, such as a particular frame geometry, a bicycle frame designed for women, or a combination of wheel size and frame size. Road and multisport models were marketed, in most cases, using 8 bicycle frame sizes. Exceptions were made for special purpose bicycles (such as, triathlon or cyclo-cross), or bicycles for women. This difference, between the number of bicycle frame sizes of these two product lines, addressed crucial needs arising from bicycle usage. Road and multisport models were mainly used for racing or fast fitness riding, and needed a bicycle frame geometry aimed at strengthening aerodynamics. As a result, the fit between the cyclist and the bicycle was a key feature to achieve a high performance in pedalling. This, in turn, required a large number of bicycle frame sizes in order to accommodate most of the customers. The urban and leisure product line presented, in most cases, 4 sizes of bicycle frame. Exceptions were made for bicycles designed for women or for wheel size. The latter example is a bicycle, using a set of 20-inch wheels, available in one size. The fluctuations in the number of bicycle frame sizes, over time,

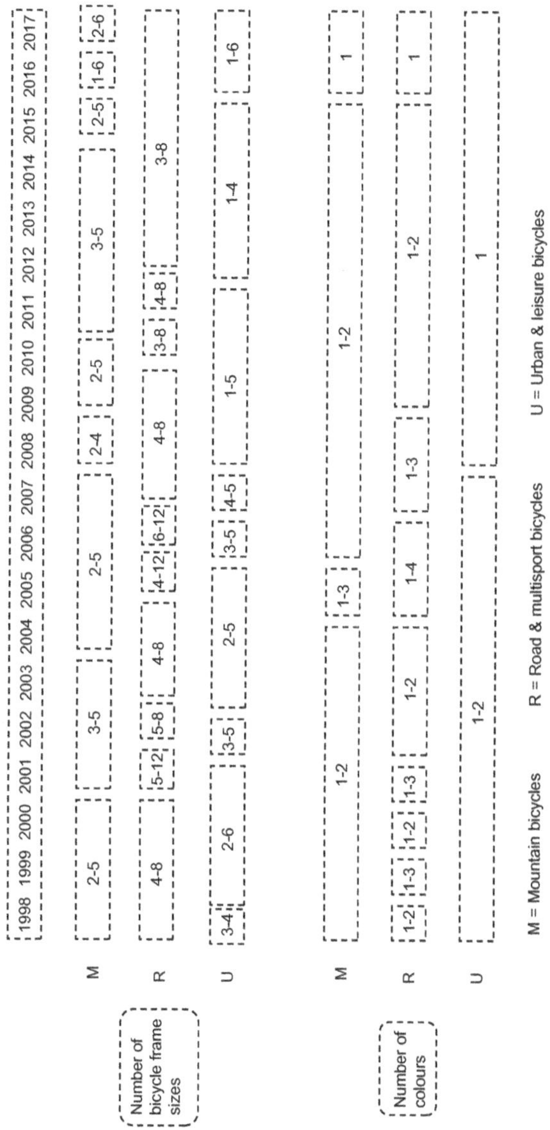

Fig. 4.5 Number of bicycle frame sizes and colours 1998–2017

are difficult to interpret without further data. Presumably, the decision to reduce or increase the number of bicycle frame sizes was based on sales data, which could help identifying customers' demands over time.

The second bicycle feature used by Cannondale to create and manage fit variety is wheel size. This specifically refers to the mountain bicycle product line as there were no significant changes to wheel size of the other two product lines from 1998 until 2017. In contrast, mountain models went through a series of variation regarding wheel size. Reasons behind this variation can be understood recalling that wheel size has marked the history of the bicycle, as discussed in the first chapter of this book, and it resurfaced in the late 2000s prompting a *wheel war* between bicycle firms manufacturing mountain bicycles. This type of bicycle was developed in the United States during the second half of the 1970s and became a product for regular production and retail distribution in 1982 (Berto 1999, pp. 69–70). Mountain bicycles used wheels of 26 inches in diameter since their introduction. The change of wheel size from 26 to 29 inches was explained as a way of improving bicycle performance in off-road riding. This is theoretically true, but there are also drawbacks, such as the increase of bicycle weight and the impact on bicycle frame geometry. It means that a bicycle, using a set of 29-inch wheels, requires a bigger frame, which exclusively fit tall cyclists. The bicycle industry had to confront with a dilemma: was a 29-inch wheel the right size for the whole mountain bicycle market? The answer was something in between a 26-inch and a 29-inch wheel. The industry developed a further wheel size of 27.5 inches, which was offered as an alternative to the 29-inch wheels. This situation put a lot of pressure on bicycle firms, which had to organize their offering around three different wheel sizes during the same year. There was a transition period of time, which saw the coexistence of the three wheel sizes. Arguing that a bigger wheel size improved the performance of cyclists did not tell the complete story. It is fair to state that changing the size of wheels was also a way to fuel the market of a product that, perhaps, needed some help to begin a new phase of its life.

Cannondale participated to the wheel war and changed its offering of mountain bicycles. Figure 4.6 depicts the main decisions made by the company since 1998. Cannondale made three types of mountain bicycles: bicycles without any suspension system (usually called rigid MTB), bicycles using a front suspension system (called front MTB), and bicycles using both a front and rear suspension system (called full MTB). Rigid

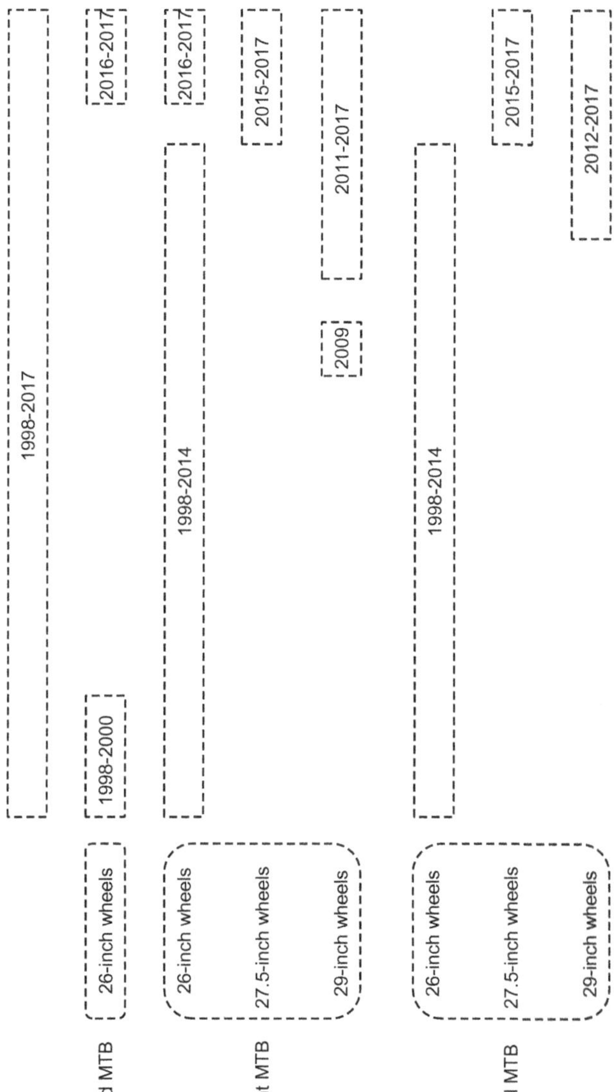

Fig. 4.6 Mountain bicycles and wheel sizes 1998–2017

mountain bicycles, using 26-inch wheels, were manufactured and sold until 2000. Front and full mountain bicycles, based on 26-inch wheels, lasted until 2014. An exception was a special model of 26-inch wheel bicycle, launched in 2016, which was available in various models, rigid and front MTBs. The first front mountain bicycle, using a set of 29-inch wheels, was introduced in 2009. It was an individual model, presumably, a test for the Italian market. In 2010, Cannondale marketed only 26-inch wheel mountain bicycles. One year later, it launched some 29-inch wheel models, based on a front suspension system. In 2012, it broadened its offering of 29-inch wheel bicycles, adding some full mountain bicycles. In 2015, Cannondale decided to increase the variety of its offering through a new wheel size. Some 27.5-inch wheel bicycles, using both front and full suspension systems, were proposed to the Italian market.

Taste variety at Cannondale was mainly carried out through colours and materials used to manufacture bicycle frames. The company adopted a parsimonious approach in managing the number of colours available for its bicycles. Figure 4.5 shows the lowest and highest number of colours available for each product line during the twenty years. Since 1998, the average number of colours per model was approximately 2 across the whole offering. There were exceptions for some mountain and road models available in 3 or 4 colours. In 2016, Cannondale decided to reduce its variety based on colours and, as a result, customers could no longer choose their preferred colour. There was just one colour available for every model. The one-colour practice was already introduced in the urban and leisure product line in 2008.

A further dimension of taste variety was the bicycle frame, particularly the material used to build it. Cannondale was a pioneer in manufacturing handmade aluminium bicycle frames and, as examined earlier, its frames were the most distinctive element of the entire offering. In 1995, the company began to design and manufacture a mountain bicycle frame using both aluminium and carbon fibres. It was a full mountain bicycle available from 1995 to 2001. Ten years later, in 2005, Cannondale presented a road bicycle frame made of carbon fibres co-moulded to aluminium. In 2006, it added its first full-carbon frame for road racing. One year later, it launched its first two mountain bicycle frames made using carbon fibres. Customers could choose to buy a front mountain or a full mountain bicycle, both based on a full-carbon frame. The same year was also available a carbon frame for urban usage. From 2008 to 2017 the carbon fibres frames significantly increased their contribution to the offering of each product lines, and potential customers had the possibility to express their taste about frame materials. Catalogues and price lists do not reveal whether carbon frames were made by Cannondale or by a supplier. The *Handmade in USA* logo did not appear on bicycles using a full-carbon frame. The manufacturing technology for building a carbon frame is very different from that of an aluminium bicycle frame. Cannondale developed a proprietary co-moulding process, but this is not the same as fabricating a full-carbon frame. What is more doubtful is the rapid increase of models based on carbon frames, which might imply an outside source for this component.

Taste variety was also granted by the introduced of further options, which customers could choose when they ordered a bicycle through the specialty bicycle retail channel. For instance, in 1998–1999, some models offered the possibility to select a different set of wheels or shift levers. After 1999, Cannondale discontinued the practice of options, presumably, because its impact on the number of product variants could be not viable in the long run.

In examining taste variety, it should be underlined that the one of the dimension of fit variety, examined earlier, can also affect the taste of potential customers. The wheel war made available alternative wheel sizes for very similar bicycles, and customers could choose which one was better for them. From 2011 until 2014, Cannondale's customers could compare a 26-inch and a 29-inch wheel bicycle. Later, from 2015 to 2017, the comparison was between a 27.5-inch and a 29-inch wheel bicycle (Fig. 4.6).

The third type of variety refers to variation in quality levels of bicycles and it shows a price-performance link between the models in the same product line. As a result, the price of a bicycle becomes a simple way to infer the quality of that product. Managing variety through prices also reflects a market segmentation approach, as discussed in the previous chapter, which allows to address differences in buying power of potential customers. Cannondale practised quality variety through a joint decision of extending its product lines and developing price tiers for each of them. It is possible to show the evolution of quality variety, during the twenty years, through data drawn from catalogues and price list. For the sake of clarity, all bicycle prices are nominal prices and represent manufacturer's suggested retail prices. They are not adjusted for inflation since understanding the impact of inflation is beyond the scope of the chapter. Data are presented for individual product line using a chart that highlights the number of models available, every year, within a particular price tier. The price tiers are organized into separate rows of 499 euro each, from the lowest to the highest bicycle price. Exceptions are the beginning and ending of this price tier arrangement. In some cases it is shown the particular price of the most affordable or the most expensive bicycle, rather than the entire price tier. It is useless to include a further price tier when there is just one model or a few models marketed at exactly the same price. Each price tier ends in 9 since this is the way used by Cannondale to set its price list. Price endings can influence the perception of potential customers. For example, prices ending in 9 are often perceived as a better deal than prices ending in other digits.

During the twenty years, mountain bicycle product line evolved from a 10-price tier range, in 1998, to a 20-price tier range, in 2017 (Fig. 4.7). This result was related to the significant increase in the number of models, which raised by 1.6 times in the same years. Since 1998 throughout 2009, Cannondale used between 8 and 12 price tiers. Form 2010, the number of price tiers continuously increased and reached its peak in 2017. The first price tier, from 449 to 499 euro, is smaller than the others, but it is worth keeping it in a separate row to highlight that Cannondale did not market mountain bicycles below 500 euro for a long time. It entered this price tier through the launch of two models at 499 euro, just for one year in 2010. It decided to re-enter the affordable price tier, in 2017, presenting five models, three of them at 499 euro and two at 449 euro. The last two tiers show the precise prices of the most expensive models of mountain bicycles. There were 4 models, in 2016, at almost 11,000 euro, and one model at almost 12,000, in 2017. These models are considered the elite-level bicycles and are called the *halo bicycles* (Anonymous 2018). They play a special role within the offering of a bicycle firm. They do not necessarily contribute to the sales of the company, but they do help build a brand identity. These bicycles are the flagship of a brand usually involved in racing as a marketing tool. Halo bicycles offer the latest technology based on weight savings and improved performance. Potential customers, who cannot afford to pay a huge amount of money for a halo bicycle, aspire to own even a fraction of such technology in buying a mid-price model or an entry-level model. Figure 4.7 shows that it is possible to identify further halo bicycles in every year from 1998 to 2017. The prices were very different from those of the two previous examples, but the bicycles were in the offering to create a halo effect. For instance, the halo bicycle of 1998 was included within the 5500–5999 price tier. In 2003,

Bicycle price (Euro)	1998	1999	2000	2001	2002	2003	2004	2005	2006	2007	2008	2009	2010	2011	2012	2013	2014	2015	2016	2017
11,999																				1
10,999																			3	1
9,500-9,999																		2		1
9,000-9,499															1	1				
8,500-8,999																1	1	1		1
8,000-8,499													1	2	2	1	1			1
7,500-7,999						1					1	1	1		1		1		4	1
7,000-7,499									2	2				1						1
6,500-6,999					1	1	1	2				1	1				2	5	2	1
6,000-6,499		1		1						2	1	1			4	2	1			
5,500-5,999	1		1	2		1	1	1	4	1	1	4	2	2	1	1		1	2	3
5,000-5,499			1			1	1	3	1	3	1			2		1	2	1	4	1
4,500-4,999	2	2	1	3		2	2		1		2	5	3	1	2	1		4	5	5
4,000-4,499	1		6	1	2	2	1	1	4	4	3			2	4	4	3	1	1	2
3,500-3,999	2	6	2	2	4	2	2	2				4	5	2	3	6	2		4	4
3,000-3,499	2		4	6	2	2	1	1	7	5	4	3	2	3	2	4	2	3	9	6
2,500-2,999	2	4	3	2	2	3	5	4	6	6	3	7	6	4	4	4	3	4	10	7
2,000-2,499	6	5	4	3	4	2	3	5	6	10	7	5	7	6	7	7	3	2	5	4
1,500-1,999	3	5	4	4	3	4	4	5	10	5	3	7	4	3	5	3	4	3	7	3
1,000-1,499	8	6	3	1	3	3	3	4	5	5	5	7	4	2	5	5	4	6	6	7
500-999	3	2	1				2	2	2	2	9	9	5	9	6	8	8	11	9	23
449-499													2							5

Years

Fig. 4.7 Models and prices of mountain bicycles 1998–2017

the price tier was between 7500 and 7999. The trend of halo bicycle prices, during the time series, is clearly moving upward. On the opposite side, it can also be seen a downward trend focused on increasing the number of more affordable models, particularly below 1000 euro. In 2017, potential customers could choose 23 different mountain bicycles marketed between 500 and 999 euro, the largest offering of the twenty years. The mountain product line was mainly concentrated within six price tiers. From 1998 to 2017, approximately 50% of the models were available at a price between 500 and 2499 euro, whereas a further 15% of models was marketed at a price ranging between 2500 and 3499 euro.

The road and multisport product line shows a similar pattern to that of the mountain bicycles. The number of price tiers increased from 7, in 1998, to 12, in 2017 (Fig. 4.8). It was steady until 2002, and then began to raise reaching a peak of 15 tiers, in 2015. The number of models increased by 3.0 times, during the twenty years, and was higher than that of mountain bicycles. A partial explanation is that road cycling, and particularly road racing, has a much longer history than mountain biking. Figure 4.8 shows that Cannondale did not offer any road bicycle below 500 euro, even though it increased its offering of more affordable bicycles below 1499 euro since the early 2010s. The halo bicycles were available each year, playing their role of show-pieces, through the sponsorship of professional road cycling teams, participating to the main races, such as the Tour de France and the Giro d'Italia. In 1998 a halo bicycle was marketed at a price range between 4000 and 4499 euro. Twenty years later, the price range became between 10,500 and 10,999 euro. The peak was reached in 2008, when a model of road bicycle was marketed at almost 12,000 euro. Most of the road and multisport bicycles are concentrated within three price tiers ranging from 1000 to 2499 euro. These bicycles accounted for approximately 50% of the models during the 1998–2017 time frame. A further 20% is available at a price ranging from 2500 and 3499 euro.

The third product line, urban and leisure bicycles, still employed the price tier approach, even though there were evident differences from the previous product lines. Firstly, the number of price tiers was almost steady during the twenty years, and was also smaller (Fig. 4.9). The average number of tiers was 5, ranging from 3 to 7. From 1998 to 2017, the number of models increased approximately by 0.9 times. Cannondale did not offer affordable urban bicycles below 500 euro. In 2017, it changed its product policy and introduced two models at 499 euro.

Bicycle price (Euro)	1998	1999	2000	2001	2002	2003	2004	2005	2006	2007	2008	2009	2010	2011	2012	2013	2014	2015	2016	2017
11,999											1									
10,500-10,999																	1		1	1
10,000-10,499															1					
9,500-9,999											1		1			1	1	1	2	
9,000-9,499										1										
8,500-8,999										1		1			1	2	1	1		
8,000-8,499									1				1		1					
7,500-7,999									1		1	1	1	1		1	1		1	2
7,000-7,499									1				1					2		
6,500-6,999								1			1	2	1	1				1	2	4
6,000-6,499							2		2	1							1		1	
5,500-5,999						1		2	2	2	2	1		1	1	2	1	2		
5,000-5,499					1	1	1	1	1			1	1		1	2		1		
4,500-4,999				2	1	1	1		1	2	2	1	1	2	1	1	4	1	6	5
4,000-4,499	1	2	1	1	2	1	1				2				2			3	2	2
3,500-3,999	2	1	1			1		3	2	3	2	4	2	4	1	7	6	2	3	7
3,000-3,499	1	1	2	2		5	2	1	3	4	3	4	2	2	2	3	4	4	6	7
2,500-2,999	2	4	2	2	4	2	1	3	3	3	2	4	2	8	8	7	4	6	9	10
2,000-2,499	3	4	6	8	3	6	5	3	7	9	7	6	6	4	8	3	8	5	10	9
1,500-1,999	3	4	5	8	7	10	8	5	5	6	9	5	6	5	4	10	2	5	8	8
1,000-1,499	5	6	4	2	3	1	5	5	7	9	5	8	9	4	8	11	9	11	10	12
500-999						2	1				2	5	3	4	1	1	2	1	1	2

Years

Fig. 4.8 Models and prices of road & multisport bicycles 1998–2017

Bicycle price (Euro)	1998	1999	2000	2001	2002	2003	2004	2005	2006	2007	2008	2009	2010	2011	2012	2013	2014	2015	2016	2017
4,599					1															
3,765				1																
3,000-3,499				2		1	1	1	3	4	2	1	1	2						
2,500-2,999				1	1	1				1	1	2	2	1					1	1
2,000-2,499	2	3	2	4	6	6	2	3	2					1	1	1	1			
1,500-1,999	2	3	4	4	9	4	9	6	11	19	13	16	9	10	6	4	4	6	7	5
1,000-1,499	7	12	9	5	6	6	9	8	16	28	15	11	9	10	12	9	4	5	7	5
500-999	7	4	4	2		2	5	3	3	2	19	20	16	13	12	16	8	11	15	21
499																				2

Years

Fig. 4.9 Models and prices of urban & leisure bicycles 1998–2017

There were expensive bicycles within this product line, however they did not resemble the idea of a halo bicycle, since the usage of urban and leisure bicycles is very different from that of the other product lines, and potential customers were unlike as well. These costly bicycles were high-performance models based on high quality bicycle frames and components. Their number was reduced since 2012. The prices of urban bicycles were concentrated between 500 and 1499 euro. Approximately 65% of them was within these two price tiers from 1998 to 2017. A further share of approximately 20% was marketed at a price ranging from 1500 to 1999 euro.

The data regarding the three product lines and their variety, during twenty years, show that Cannondale employed bicycle frame sizes as the key fit variety dimension to address customers' needs and wants. A further dimension of fit variety was added for mountain bicycles, based on wheel sizes. This latter dimension also influenced the taste variety of customers interested in mountain product line. In addition, the company extended its offering of frame materials to include carbon fibres in each product line, so as to accommodate the tastes of a broader customer base. Cannondale also decided that colours were not employed any more as a taste variety dimension. Lastly, price tiers were the crucial dimension of quality variety to approach the price sensitivity of customers.

4.4 Conclusion

The illustration of Cannondale experience in marketing its bicycles provides a valuable source for understanding how bicycle firms deal with marketing concept and tools. Despite the limited data, this chapter sheds light on marketing practices carried out by a leading company that contributed to the recent history of the bicycle industry in the United States and elsewhere.

The time series of twenty years helped to partially follow the evolution of its product policy in Italy, and it indicates that a historical analysis of bicycle industry and its marketing practices is very useful for a twofold purpose. Firstly, this type of endeavour might contribute to fill in the gap of knowledge, regarding a neglected topic and a forgotten industry. Secondly, a historical perspective could also produce a more critical interpretation of facts and events, which, in turn, could become a basis for making future decisions, and hopefully, preventing from repeating the same errors.

Cannondale experience is also instrumental in corroborating the thesis that the bicycle industry has not changed its marketing practices since its inception. This does not mean that changes are always necessary or better than the current situation. It is simply a call for not taking for granted what the bicycle industry has been doing for a long period of time. It is interesting to highlight that very recently (Frothingham 2020), Cannondale announced its decision to replace the traditional model year structure with a version that aligns with the calendar year. In other words, it means that the seasonal cycle, examined in the first chapter of this book, starting in September of every year and ending in August of the next year, is going to be replaced with an annual cycle starting in January and ending in December. It also means that the annual model change is not affected by this decision. This small change is a symptom that, perhaps, the bicycle industry is gradually building a commitment for introducing broader and more impactful improvements to its marketing activity. If the bicycle industry contributed to shape marketing practices since the early twentieth century, it is now time for a renewed interest in developing a more sustainable way of conducting marketing.

References

Anonymous. (2018). Why do bikes cost more than motorcycles? *Mountain Bike Action, 33*(4), 28–31.

Berto, F. J. (1999). *The birth of dirt: Origins of mountain biking*. San Francisco, CA: Van der Plas Publications.

Cannondale Corporation. (1973). *Backpacking and bicycling Cannondale*. Stamford, CT: Cannondale Corporation.

Cannondale Corporation. (1983). *Cannondale 1983*. Georgetown, CT: Cannondale Corporation.

Cannondale Corporation. (1988). *Cannondale 1989*. Georgetown, CT: Cannondale Corporation.

Cannondale Corporation. (1992). *Cannondale 1993*. Georgetown, CT: Cannondale Corporation.

Cannondale Corporation. (1995). *Cannondale 1996*. Georgetown, CT: Cannondale Corporation.

Cannondale Corporation. (1997a). *Cannondale 1998*. Bethel, CT: Cannondale Corporation.

Cannondale Corporation. (1997b). *Cannondale price list 1998*. Bethel, CT: Cannondale Corporation.

Cannondale Corporation. (1998a). *Cannondale 1999*. Bethel, CT: Cannondale Corporation.

Cannondale Corporation. (1998b). *Cannondale price list 1999*. Bethel, CT: Cannondale Corporation.

Cannondale Corporation. (1999a). *Cannondale 2000*. Bethel, CT: Cannondale Corporation.

Cannondale Corporation. (1999b). *Cannondale price list 2000*. Bethel, CT: Cannondale Corporation.

Cannondale Corporation. (2000a). *Cannondale 2001*. Bethel, CT: Cannondale Corporation.

Cannondale Corporation. (2000b). *Cannondale price list 2001*. Bethel, CT: Cannondale Corporation.

Cannondale Corporation. (2001a). *Cannondale 2002*. Bethel, CT: Cannondale Corporation.

Cannondale Corporation. (2001b). *Cannondale price list 2002*. Bethel, CT: Cannondale Corporation.

Cannondale Corporation. (2002a). *2001 annual report*. Bethel, CT: Cannondale Corporation.

Cannondale Corporation. (2002b). *Cannondale 2003*. Bethel, CT: Cannondale Corporation.

Cannondale Corporation. (2002c). *Cannondale price list 2003*. Bethel, CT: Cannondale Corporation.

Cannondale Corporation. (2003a). *Cannondale 2004*. Bethel, CT: Cannondale Corporation.

Cannondale Corporation. (2003b). *Cannondale price list 2004*. Bethel, CT: Cannondale Corporation.

Cannondale Bicycle Corporation. (2004a). *Cannondale 2005*. Bethel, CT: Cannondale Bicycle Corporation.

Cannondale Bicycle Corporation. (2004b). *Cannondale price list 2005*. Bethel, CT: Cannondale Bicycle Corporation.

Cannondale Bicycle Corporation. (2005a). *Cannondale 2006*. Bethel, CT: Cannondale Bicycle Corporation.

Cannondale Bicycle Corporation. (2005b). *Cannondale price list 2006*. Bethel, CT: Cannondale Bicycle Corporation.

Cannondale Bicycle Corporation. (2006a). *Cannondale 2007*. Bethel, CT: Cannondale Bicycle Corporation.

Cannondale Bicycle Corporation. (2006b). *Cannondale urban line 2007*. Bethel, CT: Cannondale Bicycle Corporation.

Cannondale Bicycle Corporation. (2006c). *Cannondale price list 2007*. Bethel, CT: Cannondale Bicycle Corporation.

Cannondale Bicycle Corporation. (2007a). *Cannondale 2008*. Bethel, CT: Cannondale Bicycle Corporation.

Cannondale Bicycle Corporation. (2007b). *Cannondale urban line 2008*. Bethel, CT: Cannondale Bicycle Corporation.
Cannondale Bicycle Corporation. (2007c). *Cannondale price list 2008*. Bethel, CT: Cannondale Bicycle Corporation.
Cannondale Bicycle Corporation. (2008a). *Cannondale 2009*. Bethel, CT: Cannondale Bicycle Corporation.
Cannondale Bicycle Corporation. (2008b). *Cannondale price list 2009*. Bethel, CT: Cannondale Bicycle Corporation.
Cannondale Bicycle Corporation. (2009a). *Cannondale 2010*. Bethel, CT: Cannondale Bicycle Corporation.
Cannondale Bicycle Corporation. (2009b). *Cannondale price list 2010*. Bethel, CT: Cannondale Bicycle Corporation.
Cannondale Bicycle Corporation. (2010a). *Cannondale 2011*. Bethel, CT: Cannondale Bicycle Corporation.
Cannondale Bicycle Corporation. (2010b). *Cannondale price list 2011*. Bethel, CT: Cannondale Bicycle Corporation.
Cannondale Bicycle Corporation. (2011a). *Cannondale 2012*. Bethel, CT: Cannondale BicycleCorporation.
Cannondale Bicycle Corporation. (2011b). *Cannondale price list 2012*. Bethel, CT: Cannondale Bicycle Corporation.
Cannondale Bicycle Corporation. (2012a). *Cannondale 2013*. Bethel, CT: Cannondale Bicycle Corporation.
Cannondale Bicycle Corporation. (2012b). *Cannondale price list 2013*. Bethel, CT: Cannondale Bicycle Corporation.
Cannondale Bicycle Corporation. (2013a). *Cannondale 2014*. Bethel, CT: Cannondale Bicycle Corporation.
Cannondale Bicycle Corporation. (2013b). *Cannondale price list 2014*. Bethel, CT: Cannondale Bicycle Corporation.
Cannondale Bicycle Corporation. (2014a). *Cannondale 2015*. Wilton, CT: Cannondale Bicycle Corporation.
Cannondale Bicycle Corporation. (2014b). *Cannondale price list 2015*. Wilton, CT: Cannondale Bicycle Corporation.
Cannondale Bicycle Corporation. (2015a). *Cannondale 2016*. Wilton, CT: Cannondale Bicycle Corporation.
Cannondale Bicycle Corporation. (2015b). *Cannondale price list 2016*. Wilton, CT: Cannondale Bicycle Corporation.
Cannondale Bicycle Corporation. (2016a). *Cannondale 2017*. Wilton, CT: Cannondale Bicycle Corporation.
Cannondale Bicycle Corporation. (2016b). *Cannondale price list 2017*. Wilton, CT: Cannondale Bicycle Corporation.
Dorel Industries Inc. (2008). *2007 annual report*. Montreal, QC, Canada: Dorel Industries Inc.

Dorel Industries Inc. (2010). *2009 annual report*. Montreal, QC, Canada: Dorel Industries Inc.

Dorel Industries Inc. (2011). *Annual report 2010*. Montreal, QC, Canada: Dorel Industries Inc.

Dorel Industries Inc. (2012). *Annual report 2011*. Montreal, QC, Canada: Dorel Industries Inc.

Dorel Industries Inc. (2013). *2012 annual report*. Montreal, QC, Canada: Dorel Industries Inc.

Dorel Industries Inc. (2014). *2013 annual report*. Montreal, QC, Canada: Dorel Industries Inc.

Dorel Industries Inc. (2015). *2014 annual report*. Montreal, QC, Canada: Dorel Industries Inc.

Dorel Industries Inc. (2016). *2015 annual report*. Montreal, QC, Canada: Dorel Industries Inc.

Dorel Industries Inc. (2017). *2016 annual report*. Montreal, QC, Canada: Dorel Industries Inc.

Dorel Industries Inc. (2018). *2017 annual report*. Montreal, QC, Canada: Dorel Industries Inc.

Dorel Industries Inc. (2019). *2018 annual report*. Montreal, QC, Canada: Dorel Industries Inc.

Dorel Industries Inc. (2020). *2019 annual report*. Montreal, QC, Canada: Dorel Industries Inc.

Frothingham, S. (2020, July). Calendar year product cycle set for Cannondale. *Bicycle Retailer and Industry News*, pp. 1, 20.

Hartford, J. (2003). *Cannondale completes chapter 11 sale to Pegasus*. Louisville, KY: SGB Media.

Montgomery, J. S. (2003). *Open letter from Cannondale concerning bankruptcy*. Bethel, CT: Cannondale Corporation.

Norman, J. (2008, February 4). Dorel buys Cannondale. *Bicycle Retailer and Industry News*.

Stone, R. A. (1998). Cannondale corporation and the mountain bike industry. In A. A. Thompson & A. J. Strickland (Eds.), *Strategic management: Concepts and cases* (10th ed., pp. 488–518). New York, NY: Irwin/McGraw-Hill.

Ulrich, K. T., Randall, T., Fisher, M., & Reibstein, D. (1998). Managing product variety. In T. Ho & C. S. Tang (Eds.), *Product variety management. Research advances* (pp. 177–205). Boston, MA: Kluwer Academic Publishers.

Correction to: Understanding the Market Through Bicycle Statistics

Correction to:
Chapter 2 in: C. Mari, *A Business History of the Bicycle Industry*, https://doi.org/10.1007/978-3-030-50563-9_2

The original version of this chapter was inadvertently published without the source line for Table 2.1 in Chapter 2, which has now been corrected. The corrections to the chapter have been updated with the changes.

The updated version of this chapter can be found at
https://doi.org/10.1007/978-3-030-50563-9_2

C. Mari, *A Business History of the Bicycle Industry*,
https://doi.org/10.1007/978-3-030-50563-9_5

Index

C. Mari, *A Business History of the Bicycle Industry*,
https://doi.org/10.1007/978-3-030-50563-9

The manufacturer's authorised representative in the EU is Springer Nature Customer Service Centre GmbH, Europaplatz 3, 69115 Heidelberg, Germany. If you have any concerns regarding our products, please contact ProductSafety@springernature.com

Printed and bound by CPI Group (UK) Ltd, Croydon, CR0 4YY

30/09/2026

02225260-0008